For Meg Healy the
who graces
right side. of
the river!

Evelyn Oppenheim

April '69

RED
RIVER
DUST

• TRUE TALES OF AN •

TRUE TALES OF AN

RED

RIVER

DUST

AMERICAN YESTERDAY

• AMERICAN YESTERDAY •

By
EUGENE W. BOWERS
and
EVELYN OPPENHEIMER

Introduction by
FRANK X. TOLBERT

WORD BOOKS, Publishers
Waco, Texas

Grateful acknowledgment is made to Harper
& Row, Publishers, for permission to quote
from David Lavender, *The Rockies,* Harper
& Row, 1968.

To the memory of
Eugene Bowers Russell
son of Mr. and Mrs. E. K. Russell
and grandson of
Mr. and Mrs. E. W. Bowers
of Clarksville, Texas

INTRODUCTION

I was surprised when I heard that these two had written a book together: Eugene W. Bowers, in my opinion Texas' most diligent cracker-barrel historian, and Evelyn Oppenheimer, one of the nation's most respected literary authorities, an intellectual and author of the bible on book reviewing.

I couldn't have been more surprised if I'd read on some publisher's list that Lady Bird Johnson and golfer Arnold Palmer were co-authors of a book.

And yet after reading *Red River Dust* it is obvious that Miss Openheimer and Mr. Bowers are quite a team! I don't want to fall completely into stately apostrophes, but this is a good book, one that should have been written, and the contrasting personalities of the co-authors light up the pages.

That part of the Red River Valley of most ancient Anglo settlement is lucky. It's too bad that other political districts don't have a Eugene Bowers and Evelyn Oppenheimer to gather up the stories of the past and to collaborate on writing them honestly and not in the chauvinistic, don't-offend-anyone manner of most county histories.

Besides having an inquisitive and orderly mind, Mr. Bowers had another immense advantage of being District Clerk of Red River County from 1933 to 1957; and his father, E. M. Bowers, held that office from 1878 to 1890. So they were in the best position to be privy to what had happened in this valley.

Most folks don't know that this valley was settled by people from the United States long before the Austins ever brought their Anglo colonists into Mexican Texas, and these people were reception committees for such bravos as Sam Houston and Davy Crockett when Houston and Crockett crossed the Red River for the first times.

Mr. Bowers has kept careful record of some pretty unique things, such as information about all the steamboats sunk along the shores of the Red River over about a fifty year period.

"Few people now realize the immense steamboat traffic on the Red River from the 1820's to about 1874 when the railroads put the boats out of business," Mr. Bowers once told me. The captains and owners of these shallow draft vessels had a rough time. They had to contend with high and low water in the temperamental Red, and most of them were constantly harassed by creditors and process-serving sheriffs.

Some years ago Mr. Bowers, being the supreme historical expert around Clarksville, was sort of referee in a legal squabble over the cargo of the "whiskey boat," the "Jim Turner." The old steamer, wrecked and sunk back in the 1850's with a supposed cargo of 300 barrels of drinking whiskey, suddenly surfaced. There were stories in newspapers all over the country about this. Then a storm came and the Red River settled the case: the "Jim Turner" sank again beneath the plasma-colored waters and hasn't been sighted since, even by divers.

The early settlers of this valley were exuberant people. For instance, there was Mrs. Isabella Clark, wife of the founder of Clarksville, who was a beautiful young girl when Davy Crockett forded the Red River into Texas in the winter of 1835-36. Mrs. Clark (known as "Aunt Ibbie" in her old age) rode a horse for miles to the cabin where Crockett was spending his first night in Texas. When she arrived, the woman of the cabin asked, "What brings you here at this hour, Mrs. Clark?" Isabella replied, "My horse and your whiskey—and I want to meet Davy Crockett!"

Then there was the poet-sheriff of Red River County, William C. Young, who later became a Confederate general. As sheriff in an 1839 case involving a steamboat, the

Selman, he served a citation with a poem among the legal papers:

> "Defend us, God, I ever pray
> From kings and lords and lazy grunters,
> From knaves and dupes and office-hunters,
> From haughty priests and drunken esquires
> And all the sins of nullifiers."

What this verse had to do with steamboat litigation, I don't know. Perhaps Mr. Bowers and Miss Oppenheimer can explain.

Incidentally, the diary quotes of Eugene Bowers' Confederate relative, Will Bowers, are worth the price of this wonderful little book.

FRANK X. TOLBERT
Dallas News Columnist, author *The Day of San Jacinto, Bigamy Jones, The Staked Plain, Informal History of Texas, Dick Dowling at Sabine Pass, A Bowl of Red.*

CONTENTS

ACKNOWLEDGMENTS

The list of men and women who have given substantial aid in this effort to share a part of America's social history is so extensive that it is heartwarming as index of their interest. The aid has come in many ways and forms, such as criticism, advice, cooperation, and encouragement during the many years of research which have been involved. There is cause to marvel at the kindness and patience of these people and their help in participating in a public duty to shed light on a background so little known for over a century.

Especially fortunate was the fact that fire never destroyed any of the five courthouses of Red River County, so that access to the complete records of the district and county courts were available to co-author Eugene W. Bowers as retired clerk.

Gratitude is expressed to A. L. Burford, Texarkana, for 241 letters; J. Evetts Haley, Canyon, author, historian; Frank X. Tolbert, author, historian, *Dallas Morning News* columnist; William A. Owens, author, historian, Columbia University faculty; Dr. C. L. Sonnichsen, author, historian, formerly of University of Texas at El Paso; Miss Maude Neville, *Paris* (Tex.) *News*; Dr. Herbert Gambrell, author, Southern Methodist University faculty, former president Texas State Historical Association; Dr. William R. Hogan, historian, author, Tulane University faculty; Floyd C. Shoemaker, Missouri Historical Society; U.S. District Judge T. Whitfield Davidson, Dallas; J. A. R. Moseley, Dallas; District Judge of Red River County N. L. Dalby; W. G. Vollmer, former president Texas & Pacific Railway; Elithe Hamilton Kirkland, author; Mallya Dean Billingsley.

Gratitude is expressed to the memories of Dr. E. C. Barker

of University of Texas, L. W. Kemp of Houston and San Jacinto Museum of History, Dr. W. F. Campbell (Stanley Vestal) of University of Oklahoma, Dr. Pat Ireland Nixon of San Antonio, Millard Cope of *Marshall News Messenger,* Lee Simmons of Sherman and Texas penal system, H. Bailey Carroll of Texas State Historical Association, A. Garland Adair of Texas Memorial Association, Hon. W. L. Thornton, J. Frank Dobie of University of Texas, Mrs. F. L. Woodward of Roxton, Miss Bena Clark, granddaughter of founders of Clarksville, historian-author A. W. Neville of *Paris News;* J. B. Donoho of pioneer Clarksville family 1836, Kenneth Roberts of Kennebunkport, Maine, author.

THE river [1] has always been red, the red of the earth that seeps into it, over a thousand miles of redness snaking across the high plains and then the valley of north Texas and becoming a clay-color boundary line of sand and water for southern Oklahoma and southwest Arkansas before sliding off into the mossy shadows of Louisiana on its way to the Gulf.

Red River it has always been called by the explorers who came to it from France and Spain. Rio Rojo or Rio Roxo or

---

[1] "In 1806 the United States was insisting that the upper Red River was the dividing line between Louisiana and New Mexico. So that (Zebulon) Pike could tell where the Red lay, he was given a Spanish-derived map that purported to show the sources of the stream in the Sangre de Cristo Mountains east of Taos. The original of that map had been prepared three years before in Mexico City by Alexander von Humboldt . . . (who) had relied on information derived from Bernardo de Miero y Pacheco, the cartographer who had gone into Utah with Escalante and had drawn maps of New Mexico for Anza. On his maps Miera clearly labeled the river Red, which was its local name. Today it is the Canadian . . . (which) runs into the Arkansas. . . . Hearing the name Red, most people surmised that it was the upper part of the same Red that runs into the Mississippi below Natchez. That Red, however, heads in the Texas panhandle, far east of the mountains." From *The Rockies,* David Lavender (New York: Harper and Row, Publishers, 1968).

Riviere Rouge was written on the old maps. Only a hundred years ago it became officially Red River in English or the reasonable facsimile which was spoken along its course.

If a woman is a sometime thing, so is a river, It can be just as variable in mood, just as nervous and unpredictable in movement. Especially this one.

At times its course was a torrent, and at other times a trickle. But always it was treacherous due to the currents and quicksands which swallowed many a man and his horse, a steer, an ox and wagon in the days before the bridges.

Even so, men from the north crossed it at what they called Pecan Point and Old Jonesboro, men like Davy Crockett and Sam Houston. For awhile none of them knew for sure if the Red or the Sulphur River was the boundary he was seeking to cross, because after the Louisiana Purchase the officials in Washington failed to make this detail quite clear.

But what did it matter? Once a man crossed the Red he knew that he was a far piece from Washington and anything official. He was on his own among the pines and postoak and bois d'arc trees. Crossing the Big Red was what mattered and not whether he was in Arkansas or Missouri or Mexican Texas.

In 1836 the valley had a name created out of nothing but the most natural logic: Red River County. What else could it have been? The settlers were already oldtimers there before Stephen F. Austin brought his first colonists into Texas hundreds of miles to the south of them. A second generation was already growing up and listening to "the hoot owls holler at noon" where folks said that they used possums for watchdogs.

Red River was a county as big as many a state or country. It covered so much of northeast Texas when Texas became a Republic that today there are some thirty counties which were once a part of that original Red River district.[2]

---

[2]Z. T. Fulmore, *History and Geography of Texas As Told By County Names,* (Austin: Steck-Vaughn, 1935. These are Archer, Baylor, Bowie, Cass, Childress, Clay, Collin, Collingsworth, Cooke, Cottle, Delta, Denton, Fannin, Foard, Franklin, Grayson, Hardeman, Haskell, Hunt, Hopkins, Jack, King, Knox, Lamar, Marion, Montague, Morris, Stonewall, Throckmorton, Titus, Wheeler, Wichita, Wilbarger, Wise, Young.

Always it seems that the people there were self-conscious of destiny. Aware of a history which was taking shape, they wrote diaries and kept records and began printing a paper as early as 1842.

Before, during, and after the coming of the steamboats and railroads, no way of life is better documented in any regional history of America's expanding frontier than in the dusty files and albums and shoeboxes of notes so carefully preserved along the Red River's southern shore.

Nor does any family possess and have access to more of a collection of those records, official and personal, than the Bowers family of Clarksville, the Red River County seat. Even a Confederate grandfather proved himself a Red River Pepys.

But it was in the old courthouses, five of them dating from 1828, that the records piled up and formed the strata of the history of a time too lively and vigorous to collect only dust. No, at first they whispered and then they spoke out in order to be heard again.

And so for the most part, those bound volumes of ordinances which were kept from 1837 on are the source of these stories of Americana, plus the diaries, papers and letters, and the memories of experience still sunset-red along the river.

Too often the past becomes enshrined in a rigid formality, so that we see only the pattern and not the people in a history, any history. Here let us have our focus on what was and is of human interest then as now, the personal elements which made men and women laugh and worry and do all the strange things which have a way of becoming forgotten footnotes and which hold a residue of entertainment or importance all their own.

In time such things form a current as directive as the river.

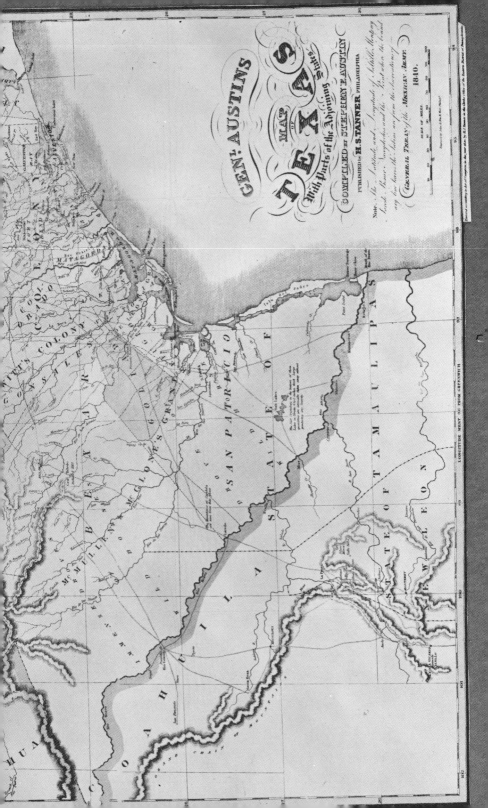

GEN'L AUSTIN'S

MAP

OF

TEXAS

With Parts of the Adjoining States

COMPILED BY STEPHEN F. AUSTIN

PUBLISHED BY H. S. TANNER PHILADELPHIA

1840.

Note.— The Latitude and Longitude by Astronomical History
Lunar Runar Amphitheas and the Positions in the Coast
are here laid down as from the Ascendency.

GENERAL TERRAY the MEXICAN BOUNDARY.

SCALE OF MILES

*The Red River County
Courthouse was built in
1881, the fifth courthouse
in Clarksville. When co-
author Eugene Bowers re-
tired as clerk of the District
Court in Clarksville, the
Senate of Texas passed the
resolution honoring him
(left).*

1.

The Judge's Dilemma

WITH the Red River valley as the only entry into Texas from the north, inevitably a town had to develop which would be an outpost of frontier society and facilities, a jumping-off place into the wilderness south and west.

In the early nineteenth century such a town took shape known as Clarksville, named for the pioneer James Clark family who founded it. On an 1841 map it was the only town marked in all northeast Texas.

With the only courthouse and as the only judicial district in over two hundred miles, naturally this area became a mecca for young lawyers alert to adventure and opportunity. It also had its attractions for older men who had their reasons for posting signs on the doors of homes and offices east of the Mississippi, "G.T.T." (Gone To Texas).

Litigation was endless over land and boundary disputes, slaves, debts, supply shipments, etc., and the courthouse was constantly being outgrown. The first one was simply the second story of a general store, sixteen miles northwest on the river at Old Jonesboro. That was in 1828 and it was called the Courthouse of Miller County, Arkansas, because at the time this region was thought to be in Arkansas.

In 1837 a move was made to the village of La Grange, six miles away. Then eight months later came the move into the county seat's newly built log structure in the public square at Clarksville. Later, of course, the courthouse there was to be rebuilt and enlarged into brick and stone buildings twice again until a size big enough to be permanent was reached.

But it was the old log cabin courthouse that was Judge John Hansford's destination on the morning of March 23, 1840, as he walked out of the Western Star Hotel.

As usual when court was in session, both the square and the courthouse were overflowing with litigants and lawyers. Among the dozens of lawyers in Clarksville's six to seven hundred population there were men who had signed the Declaration of Independence for the Republic of Texas and future Supreme Court Judges, all of them creators of a new body of legal tradition. There were also the usual scalawags, shysters, and opportunists who thronged a frontier.

It was going to be another strenuous day's work, and when His Honor, Judge Hansford took his place on the bench and began calling his docket, he was duly thankful for having had the foresight to stop and fortify himself with a little after-breakfast bourbon at the Imperial Saloon. Such a brief pause for preparation was not only customary but also practical necessity on a day like this.

Of course it had been a momentary unpleasantness when one of the town drunks, Charlie Rowland, had accosted him in the saloon, protesting a recent jail sentence. But incidents like that were customary too. The Hon. John Hansford erased Charlie's threats from his mind and got down to the business of the Seventh Judicial District of Texas.

His first case was for a divorce, John Nall vs. Catherine Nall. This was rare enough to hold special interest. Divorce cases almost never appeared on a frontier docket. Women were too scarce and valued too highly, regardless of their looks or disposition. When a man was able to get a wife, he held on to her very literally for better or for worse. Obviously John Nall in this case had suffered beyond all endurance.

Therefore, after the jury gave its verdict in favor of freedom for the afflicted husband, it was with more than a usual flourish that Judge Hansford wrote the judgment in the full legal formality of the day.

"It is therefore decreed that the said John Nall be forever divorced from the said Catherine Nall *A Vincula Matrimoni,* as well as *A Musa et Thoro,* and that the said parties be at liberty to intermarry with any other person the same as if no such marriage had ever taken place. And that the plaintiff pay all costs in this case having accrued with exception of a Tax Fee."

After this effort His Honor leaned back in his chair and, as was his habit, rested his hand in a chink between the logs of the wall at his back.

Many cases had been tried before Judge Hansford through the sessions of court when it was held here, and much resting of his hand in that particular chink had gradually worn a hole all the way through the wall. As a result the Judge's hand could, would, and did dangle outside the wall.

It was just at such a moment when Charlie Rowland staggered out of the saloon. Artfully dodging a few horses and some stray cattle and hogs on the street, he managed to cross it and steered his way around the courthouse to the back.

Not even his alcoholic content could help him to comprehend what he saw there. No wall of a building was supposed to have a human hand protruding from it. Or was it human?

Fascinated with both horror and interest, he drew closer to study the phenomenon. Definitely it was human. Definitely it was hairy, rugged, male.

Precariously Charlie leaned over for still closer examination. Slowly but surely his foggy mind registered recognition of this hand, for on a finger was a signet ring he remembered staring at when he got his last sentence from Judge Hansford.

Here was his chance not to temper justice with mercy. Charlie let out one good hiccup, opened his mouth, and clamped down on that hand with a bite and held on more fiercely than any bulldog.

Inside the courtroom the Judge gave a yell of sheer agony. The yell became a series of howls and curses. Court was, so to speak, adjourned.

After one look at close range the sheriff saw that His Honor was not having a fit but was attached to external evidence. He ran outside, raced around the courthouse, and tore the culprit loose.

After all possible first aid to both parties, the distinguished lawyers present searched the statutes, but all they could find to cover this crime which had so sorely affected both the Judge and the dignity of the court was "simple assault."

Accordingly, Charlie was fined $24.80, including costs. Unable to pay it, he served it out in jail as usual.

But after that it was noted that Judge Hansford always presided at court with his hands in his pockets.

2.

Star Navy

I T was so long ago that a can of salmon cost only a dime. A tin of northern fish like that was a tasty treat and change from Red River catfish. But first you had to have the dime, ten good solid American cents. The Hall boy did not have a penny, much less ten, and that's what caused the trouble.

It was a Sunday night, and most of the village of Manchester were at the Baptist Church listening to a sermon as hot as the weather. The windows were all broken and that helped the ventilation, that and the men fanning with their big straw hats.

Flies buzzed in and mosquitoes hummed. This the preacher and congregation were used to, but suddenly something else came in and with a resounding "splut" hit Brother Snell squarely between the eyes. It was as big a "chaw" of tobacco as anybody had ever seen, and juicy wet.

His face dripping tobacco juice, Brother Snell let out a curse of all hell fire and ran to the windows, but all he could see and hear was a hound dog running and barking after some fast disappearing figures.

This was serious. It was a case of disturbing public worship. Besides, it had made him curse in church, a talent usually exhibited only to his family.

Several men and women said that they had seen Pink Shorter outside the window before the "chaw" was launched, so Brother Snell went to Squire Holmes and swore out a complaint against Pink for arrest.

The date for trial was set, and Pink came into Clarksville to engage Brother Worley, a combination lawyer and preacher, to defend his innocence. County Attorney Jones went to Manchester to represent the State, a jury was summoned, and most of the population were subpoenaed as witnesses.

The evidence, carefully preserved but rapidly drying, was examined by a number of expert tobacco chewers. Unanimously they declared it to be "Star Navy" brand, famous for the frontier adage, "Chew Star Navy, Spit Ham Gravy."

At once the defense called upon the local merchants, who testified that Pink never bought "Star Navy." His chew was always "New Hope.".

Then came the climax of the defense, as it was demonstrated that from where Pink was alleged to have stood outside that window, it was a physical impossibility for him to have hit Brother Snell without throwing a curve.

Several veterans were called upon to attempt this feat, but none could turn in a performance at all satisfactory. Tobacco flew in all directions—but no curves.

The jury retired and returned almost at once with their verdict. Not guilty.

Many years later one of the Hall boys confessed. He had thrown the tobacco—by hand. He had done it because Mr. Snell refused him credit at his store for a dime can of salmon.

The moral was not that truth will out, but that it weighs heavily on a man's conscience to throw a "chaw" by hand and not by mouth.

Such are the signs of weakness which led to the breakdown of pioneer spirit.

3.

Master and Slave

SLAVERY was not a question south of the Red River. It was a problem, but only as part of a life made up of many problems. To question slavery was to have questioned a whole way of life, and if there had been a Red River Socrates, no doubt he passed away in poison oak and ignominy.

The slave trade flourished across the Red, and inevitably a tremendous body of laws and customs evolved in connection with it. In fact, the customs often took precedence over the written laws, but both very naturally were slanted to the benefit of the owners.

There was very little real system ever devised to identify slaves and to establish titles to them. They were not registered or numbered in anyway, and they had no surnames. This was the cause of a very large number of the lawsuits in Texas from 1836 to as late as 1867.

Another difficult situation arose from the fact that the slaves were moved in large groups from the old states into Texas. Such trips were long and hard by wagon and boat and on foot. Then came the matter of arranging to feed and house them until plantation sites were located in the new country.

There were men in Red River County who specialized in these projects. For a fee they would go to Arkansas or Louisiana to meet slave-owners who were moving their human cargo to Texas. Then they would take charge of the slaves and bring them across the border, giving the masters time to return home and escort their own families back. Often this was done on a credit arrangement, the agents holding the slaves as security until the owners reappeared and paid them for this service. Many lawsuits resulted from the disappearance of slaves as well as witnesses to the contracts. It was a loose way of doing business, and too many human elements were involved for any truly dependable control of those deals.

Following is a selection of stories on record which tell the tale in individual cases ranging from romance to its blood-red opposite.

* * *

First there is the story of Priscilla.

She was beautiful. She was colored and, of course, a slave.

At only eleven years old her beauty had begun attracting the attention of two men aware of the woman she would be. One was her master Charles Harrison, and the other was a business partner, David Hanley. They waited and watched her—and each other.

The girl had the softly olive complexion of the shade called "griffe" there in Water Valley, Mississippi. She was quadroon or octoroon. In either case, it was clear that her mother and grandmother had been preyed upon by white men. As result, Priscilla had the best features of both races, and her value was high.

It was in the year 1838 that Charles Harrison and David Hanley agreed to liquidate their business in Water Valley. However, they had become involved in a surety debt of several thousand dollars, and though Hanley could pay his share in cash, Harrison was unable to raise the money. At once Hanley offered to pay off the whole debt if Harrison gave him good security for later repayment.

What was known then as a "deed in trust" was executed as Harrison put up certain property for security. Among this property was a number of slaves, and in this number the young mulatto girl Priscilla was included.

For several years Harrison had met and made his payments on the debt as he sold some slaves and real estate. But late in 1843, at a time when money was tight generally, Hanley judged the time was right to express his dissatisfaction with Harrison's payments and turned the note over to an attorney to bring suit to foreclose for the unpaid balance.

Oddly enough, Charles Harrison did not appear and made no defense, so the Court of Yalobusha County, Mississippi, awarded Dave Hanley the judgment by default.

Well aware that by now Harrison owned only some livestock and three slaves, Hanley immediately had an order of sale issued commanding the sheriff to offer this property for sale at the courthouse door as soon as possible. The date was set for three weeks later.

Hanley could hardly wait for that morning to come. All that mattered to him was that Priscilla was one of these three remaining slaves. She was eighteen now, and he knew that Harrison was living with her and had been for some time. Obsessed with jealousy and desire, Hanley could be interested in no other woman, white or colored. Only Priscilla with her lithe, willowy figure, her delicately shaded skin and mellow dark eyes.

But a week before the sale was to be held, he noticed on his rides by Harrison's place that it was looking peculiarly deserted. In alarm he checked with neighbors and found that none of them had seen Harrison or Priscilla or his carriage and team of perfectly matched sorrel horses for several days. Finally a slave was found who could only report "Marse Charley and Priscilla done gone."

Official investigation proved this correct. "Done gone" too

were the carriage and sorrel team. But no investigation could find out where they had gone.

The sale of the property was duly held, and furiously Hanley bought it all far below value. Most of the men who attended the sale knew what was behind the situation, and the jokes they made at Hanley's expense added to his fury and frustration.

Three months passed, and then he got the information he was waiting for: Harrison was in Clarksville, Red River County, Texas.

At once Hanley got a transcript of the court judgment and sheriff's report of what was still owed him. Then he planned his trip to Texas.

Three routes were possible. He could go by stagecoach, a long and roundabout route. He could go to New Orleans and then by steamboat up the Mississippi and Red River to Jonesboro or Rowland, the ports serving Clarksville. He could ride or drive.

Hanley was confident now and decided to go by stagecoach. After all, he didn't want to be bothered with a horse of his own, because he would be returning with Harrison's team and carriage. The drive would be a pleasure then with Priscilla in the carriage with him.

After two weeks en route Hanley stepped off the stagecoach in front of the Donoho Hotel in Clarksville. At the time this was one of the best taverns in Texas. A couple of servants took his baggage, two massive bags known as "West Tennessee Grips" which could hold almost everything a man had except his family, slaves, livestock, and real estate.

Hanley was escorted to his room, a large one on the second floor looking out on Clarksville's public square and log courthouse. It was a busy scene that day in 1844. The town already had some 600 citizens as permanent population, and each day new people kept coming in to get outfitted and move on to wherever they decided to locate in Texas. The nearest town of comparable size was another 200 miles to the south, Nacogdoches.

For a moment Hanley watched the crowds milling around the square, then refreshed himself and hurried down to the lobby to find out what he could about Charley Harrison.

Yes, indeed, the hotel clerk knew Mr. Harrison. He was staying a block east at the Western Star Hotel. Everybody knew Mr. Harrison and that good-looking Priscilla of his. She worked in the Western Star dining room and that's why most fellows went there to eat, just to look at her pass those biscuits. But looking was all you could do, because Mr. Harrison sure saw to that.

Hanley mumbled something and let him pass. His fists were With only a casual glance at the store names he passed—Montgomery, Alexander, Wright, Shelton—he rounded the corner toward the Western Star and almost collided with a man much bigger than himself.

The man was Charles Harrison.

The two men stared at each other in startled surprise, and it was Harrison who first regained composure and spoke.

"I know why you're here," he said, "and you might as well go back to Water Valley 'cause you're sure as hell not going to get it. Now stay away from her!"

Hanley mumbled something and let him pass. His fists were clenched but he knew he was no match physically for a man of Harrison's size.

Instead he went back to the Donoho and began making more inquiries. He learned that Harrison evidently had money and was spending it in Clarksville in the form of notes on the Planters' Bank of Tennessee in Nashville. These notes were signed by both the bank's president and cashier.

Harrison had rented 200 acres of black prairie land from a man named Hopkins a couple of miles southwest from town. He was also in the process of buying three slaves and hiring several more to work the land.

Renting slaves was becoming a popular practice as many

owners, especially women, had inherited slaves instead of land. Accordingly, they rented them out to people with land to work, and an able-bodied slave could be hired for $100 a year. In these contracts of hire was the provision that "slaves are to be properly fed and be furnished with one winter suit and two summer suits of clothes, one hat and one blanket and two pairs of shoes and to pay the taxes on them and their doctor bills." Some of the contracts also stipulated that the slaves "not be put to work on Red River," and Hanley learned that this was because of the high mortality rate among slaves working directly along the river shore. The dread disease which took such a toll was malaria.

Hanley next directed his investigation to find the best legal talent available. Outstanding were Ebenezer Allen and Amos Morrill.[1] But since Allen was Attorney General of the Republic of Texas and also acting as Secretary of State, he was at his office in Clarksville only part of the time and took very few private cases anymore. But Allen happened to be here now, as luck would have it.

The other lawyer Morrill was by reputation "the toughest," and all lawyers had a healthy fear of his ruthlessness in dealing with them, their clients, and witnesses. They hated and respected him. With all this information Hanley spent a sleepless night. He was also kept awake by mosquitoes of a type he had never seen before, small and dapple-winged, with their tails pointing up in the air.

Next morning after more than his usual coffee, he went to Mr. Allen's office, which was in the hotel. He produced his papers from Mississippi and explained the suit he wanted to bring against Harrison.

Allen agreed to take the case, prepare and file the suit, but he warned Hanley that his official duties at Austin, especially in connection with the possible annexation of Texas

---

[1]Amos Morrill later became Chief Justice of the Texas Supreme Court and federal judge. He died a man of wealth with property in Dallas and fifteen other counties. See p. 88, "The Mighty Morrill," District Court Red River County, Cause No. 2121

to the United States, would keep him from the trial work. His advice was for Hanley to engage Morrill to try the case.

Hanley gladly agreed to this. From what he had heard of Morrill, he certainly preferred having him on his side.

These matters settled now, Hanley spent the rest of the day looking around town and trying to stay away from the Western Star and the sight of Priscilla.

He was surprised at how orderly and peaceful the town was. He had been told by friends at home that a trip into Texas was filled with danger. He had expected an Indian raid, but the Indians he saw, mostly Choctaws, were quietly trading at the stores like everyone else. He learned that only rarely was a white man killed by an Indian and then only because of mistreatment. Five times more Indians were killed by white men, the storekeepers told him. The Indians came in peace from across the river to trade deer hides, venison, snakeroot, and pinkroot for the white man's merchandise, mostly whiskey. When there was trouble, it was usually the whiskey that caused the trouble on both sides.

Hanley had an early supper, bought some mosquito netting, and went to his room to catch up on his sleep.

In the morning he returned to Mr. Allen's office and heard the petition which Allen had ready. With expert logic and force, it presented the legal facts and asked for a writ of sequestration on Harrison's horses, carriage, and the slave Priscilla, pending settlement of the suit.

At once Harrison was served with the citation and writ. He lost no time in going to the equally well-known law firm of Young and Scurry,[2] who heard his story and took the case

---

[2]William C. Young had been in Red River County for several years as its first sheriff, as a Texas Ranger, and then as district attorney.

In later years during the Civil War, Young became colonel of the Fourth Regiment of Texas Cavalry and fought with distinction in Arkansas and Indian Territory. On a short furlough at home in 1862, he was killed near Gainesville, Texas, by Union sympathizers. Fifteen of his murderers were caught and hanged on the same tree.

William R. Scurry became a Confederate general and was killed at the Battle of Jenkins Ferry in Louisiana, April 30, 1864.

Young and Scurry counties in west Texas were named for these men.

on grounds that the debt had been paid.

As the time approached the next week for the regular term of the District Court to be convened with Judge John T. Mills presiding, Dave Hanley became more and more worried— not about the trial, but about his health.

He was having chills and fever and severe headaches. People in the hotel began staying away from him, and Dr. Enos Look was called to see him.

Dr. Look, who also owned the drugstore where you could buy even a horse or a slave, came and took one long look at Hanley.

"Malaria."

He left a huge bottle of quinine for heroic doses at regular intervals.

By sheer will power Hanley was able to attend the opening of court with his lawyers on Monday morning, and even as ill and weak as he was, he was impressed with what he saw and heard.

Many other famous lawyers were present, including such men as General J. Pinckney Henderson, General Thomas Jefferson Rusk, Isaac Van Zandt, Nathaniel D. Ellis, and Robert Potter.

As the day wore on and cases were set and juries selected, Hanley noted a number of interesting cases involving slavery. One was an indictment against a merchant for trading with a slave without written consent of the master. Several cases involved masters who had rented slaves and were being sued by the actual owners for mistreatment.

Another case concerned a suit for slander by a man accused of stealing a cow. One man was suing an entire group of civic leaders for binding him to Page's Tree and whipping him.

It was not until Friday that the case of *Hanley vs. Harrison* was called for trial. By then the secret circumstances had leaked out, gossip was at a good tempo, and anyone who could call himself a Southern gentleman was there.

When Harrison brought Priscilla into the courtroom, there

was a mass intake of breath. Men nudged each other and eyes lighted up in admiration. Here was reason enough why several Presidents and statesmen had found similar relationships irresistible.

Priscilla sat down with quiet dignity, her own eyes veiled with all she could not say about either of the men fighting for possession of her. Whether she enjoyed or hated the body and looks which were the cause of the quarrel, none of the men present could know.

Judge Mills heard all the evidence, and his decision was that the writ of sequestration be sustained, subject to final trial. But Young and Scurry had a replevy bond ready whereby Harrison could keep Priscilla until the trial was completed. Then as a dilatory tactic they asked for a continuance until the fall season term of court, alleging that this was necessary in order to obtain depositions from persons living in Mississippi and Tennessee. Judge Mills considered this and granted it.

Hanley, of course, was enraged at such delay. He went back to his hotel room, feeling worse and worse, and again had Dr. Look examine him.

How could he have caught this damnable disease? Dr. Look explained that the answer to that was in much dispute. Theories ranged from "night air" to eating green fruit or too much wild game.[3]

Hanley made every effort to wait it out until the next court session. But the chills and fever and drenching, weakening sweats were wrecking him. He looked like the ghost of the man who had come from Mississippi just a little over a month before.

Hanley knew that Harrison was offering him a $500 settlement, and one day he managed to walk around to the Western Star and take a good long look at Priscilla as she went about her work in the dining room. He thought of his years of

---

[3]It would not be until July, 1898, that Dr. Ronald Ross, British Army surgeon and later Sir Ronald Ross, announced the Anopheles mosquito bite responsible.

waiting and all he had done and spent in time, money, effort; and now his very health was at stake. She was not worth it. No woman was. He made his decision and felt better for it. Thus can one illness counteract another.

With a spurt of strength he tottered to Harrison's room and told him that he would accept the settlement offer.

The former partners regarded each other and then suddenly smiled in understanding and shook hands. Once again they were friends as Harrison helped Hanley downstairs and up the street to the lawyer's office to execute the necessary papers.

With Harrison still helping him, Hanley returned to his room, packed his bags and got on the Little Rock Stagecoach. Again they shook hands, and as the horses took off, Harrison waved and Hanley leaned back in his seat, wearily closed his eyes, and thankfully left Texas forever.

In equal relief Harrison went to work on his new land and prospered in a moderate way. But in 1861 he came down with malaria too, and Priscilla nursed him until his death in March of that year. By then they had three children.

When Harison's will was read, she learned that he had provided for her freedom and also the freedom of the children.

Priscilla was thirty-four years old now, and her freedom became a handicap. She could not compete with slave labor. Why should anyone pay her a wage for work done by slaves?

Ironically, the only way to take care of herself and the children was through a law enacted in Texas for free men or women to appear in court and ask to be made a slave again. This she did with Amos Morrill's help as lawyer, and as the law provided for a choice of master, she chose the Alexander Johnston farm.

When the war came, Priscilla and her children stayed with the Johnstons, and after the Emancipation Proclamation they still stayed on and worked there as loyal servants until all the older members of the family were dead.

Then in 1880 the middle-aged Priscilla and her children left their strange past behind them and went to St. Louis.

There they "passed" or "crossed over" into the white man's world, the world which had produced them.

Into that world they disappeared.

*   *   *

Another story involved the Hon. John T. Mills, the judge who had presided at the hearing of the Hanley—Harrison case concerning Priscilla. Even judges themselves became entangled in the chaotic conditions of slave-trading and were in need of other lawyers to try to unravel the legal red tape which was supposed to provide for situations no man could foresee.

So many of these personal situations had to be "played by ear" that it is no wonder that much had to be dismissed and settled by compromise. Especially was this so in cases of stolen slaves, as Judge Mills discovered.

He was holding court at Boston in Bowie County, Texas, on October 18, 1845, when the adjournment for dinner came. He walked out on the street, stopped for some conversation with friends, and was introduced to a man named Argus McCarstle. McCarstle said that he was from Louisiana and had some slaves for sale.

The judge went to see them and bought a woman called Milly and her baby boy. For them he agreed to pay $500— $200 cash down payment and three notes for $100 each, payable by March of the following year.

It was a simple routine transaction, and Judge Mills thought no more about it. He went on to his dinner and back to court.

But a few days later a young man by the name of Joshua Alexander, Jr., of East Baton Rouge Parish, Louisiana, rode into town and filed charges against McCarstle for having stolen the slaves. Then Alexander took the slaves and started riding east with them.

McCarstle was arrested and put in jail. He got a lawyer, S. F. Mosely, who brought him before Judge Mills on a writ of habeas corpus. The Judge ordered him released and the case dismissed.

Then by another writ Judge Mills had the high-handed Mr. Alexander stopped before he got to the Sabine River and repossessed Milly and her child, who were the Judge's property.

Meanwhile McCarstle left town and was never heard of or from again.

The mystery of who had stolen from whom deepened, but the Judge had the woman and child he had bought and paid for.

Now, however, the lawyer Mosely came to Judge Mills with the three notes for the remaining $300 which McCarstle had endorsed and given to Mosely for getting him out of jail. Mosely demanded payment. The Judge refused. Mosely filed suit.

By this time His Honor needed a lawyer, so he engaged Amos Morrill to represent him.

At once Morrill filed an answer on the point that the endorsed notes were taken under circumstances of suspicion. The trial was set for December 21, 1846.

But long before then Joshua Alexander, Sr. came from Louisiana to Judge Mill's home in Clarksville and showed him his title to Milly and her son. The Judge had, without any way of knowing it, bought stolen slaves. Accordingly, he paid Alexander $550 for them.

Still Mosely persisted with his case and the trial had to be held. Both Alexander's son and son-in-law came to testify that the slaves in question had been stolen, so that any "sale" made by McCarstle was not legal and binding, thereby releasing the Judge. But Mosely contended that a note was a note, stolen goods or not.

The jury was out all day and reported that they still could not agree. They were discharged, and the case was tried again in 1847, 1848, and 1849, and still no jury could agree.

Finally, on the Red River County court records of May 12, 1851, this entry concerning it was made by the clerk: "Dismissed on compromise."

But what the compromise was and who made it, nobody knows.

*   *   *

Lawyers and judges were not the only experts who were tricked by the slave-traders. Officers of the law were too, men like Edward West, sheriff of Red River County.

In early October, 1843, Sheriff West met a man who gave his name as William Brewer. He told West that he had just come into Clarksville from Missouri and that he had a fine young slave, a boy called Jack, for sale. What's more, he was going to sell him at a bargain price because he needed the money for another business matter.

West was interested and went with him to the barn back of the Donoho Hotel where slaves of the hotel guests were always quartered.

He examined Jack, a strong fellow of light complexion, and saw that he was in excellent condition. A slave like that was worth at least $1,000 on the market then.

When Brewer said that he would sell the young Negro for only $600, West bought him at once, paying $200 cash and giving his note for the remainder, due six months later.

As soon as Sheriff West and the slave Jack were gone, Brewer went to his room and endorsed the note for $400 to Samuel Carter. Then he got his horse and rode out to the home of Miles Reed, who farmed six hundred acres next to the nine hundred acres of his friend and neighbor Sheriff West.

As Samuel Carter now, Brewer made a deal with Mr. Reed for a tract of land and gave West's note as part payment.

Then Brewer alias Carter returned to town, packed his bags and left.

Naturally, when the note fell due, Reed took it to West for payment. But the sheriff had his doubts now about the validity of the whole transaction and refused to pay it.

Carter (Brewer) was reported to live in Jasper County, Missouri, and West had reason to believe that the slave Jack was not a slave at all but a free man from the north who was the victim of illegal shenanigans.

Reed, however, felt that he was also a victim and filed suit against West. The case was tried first in May, 1847, and West won the verdict. Reed's lawyer Amos Morrill appealed the case and took it to the Texas Supreme Court, which reversed the decision.

Meanwhile, a Mr. John Rymon arrived in Clarksville and on December 31, 1849, filed a writ of habeas corpus to prove that Jack was definitely not a slave but a free man named Eli Terry of Marion County, Indiana.

"Jack" was brought before Judge John T. Mills, and the clerk read the following statement, sworn and attested and signed by the clerk of Marion County Circuit Court, Indiana: "I was formerly well-acquainted with a yellow man of color about 30 years of age now. This man is about 5 feet 9 inches high and his name is Eli Terry. He is the son of David Terry. He was fraudulently abducted and taken from this state about seven or eight years ago by one James Carter and conveyed by Carter into the State of Missouri and thence to Texas and there sold as a slave. For many years before the abduction of Eli I was well acquainted with his father and mother, free residents of the State of Indiana. Eli worked for more than a year as a steersman on a canal boat on the Central Canal in Indiana. He will be able to give a description of the Canal and many other things in and about the City of Indianapolis."

Another document was also presented proving that the Terry family had come to Indiana from Cumberland County, North Carolina, where they were free and of good reputation for their honesty and industry.

Eli Terry was thoroughly identified and recognized to be the so-called slave Jack, and after hearing all the evidence Judge Mills wrote on the minutes of the Court: "It is considered by this Court that Eli Terry is a free man and he is therefore discharged and set at liberty to go where he may see proper. In testimony I have hereunto set my hand and affix my official signature on this day of January 8, 1850."

And so Eli Terry walked out of the courtroom with John Rymon, his eyes bright with tears. In a few hours he was on his way home to his family in Indiana, too happy to realize that actually he was due the money for his past seven years of labor as a slave.

After all this, the *Reed vs. West* lawsuit died a natural death by mutual agreement. It had engaged eight lawyers and was tried by three district judges.

Only Shakespeare had the title for it: *All's Well That Ends Well.*

4.

Female Education

E DUCATION for the ladies was not neglected along the Red
River. It was just exclusive. It was the Pine Creek Female
Institute.

As early as 1841, Robert and Martha Washington Weatherred were conducting this boarding school with classes "in
Philosophy, Astronomy, Rhetoric, Composition, Logic and
Chemistry." That was a busy year for Mrs. Weatherred, for
in addition to imparting such a variety of instruction to the
young ladies of pioneer families, she also bore a son who was
to become a senator of prominence in drafting the bill for
building the future state capitol.

Undaunted by past, present, or future, however, the Weatherreds had built their Pine Creek Female Institute on land
belonging to a man named Will Mays about fifteen miles
northwest of Clarksville. Unfortunately, the main record of
their academic efforts is in several lawsuits among the district
court files of Red River County which reveal what a financial
struggle they had.

In the spring of 1843 Mr. Mays sued Prof. Weatherred for

a debt of $251.12. This was itemized to include 551 pounds of bacon for the previous two years, 99 pounds of lard, 126 pounds of soap, 27 pounds of sugar, 48 pounds of butter, 100 bushels of corn, 3½ pounds of coffee (obviously from this small amount, not their favorite beverage), 7 dozen eggs, medicines, 1 pair of shoes (evidently that pair had to last three years, as they were bought in 1841), and the boarding of two young lady students at the Mays home. In addition was the charge for rental on the schoolhouse.

In answer the harried teacher filed a bill against Mays for the tuition of the Mays children and for the use of the Weatherred "waggon and team," plus carpentry work which the schoolmaster had done for Mays on a cotton gin and press, and fixing flooring, windows, doors, bedsteads, locks, stairways, and a coffin. The total on these items came to $284.74.

When the case was tried, the jury's verdict was in favor of the teacher-carpenter. Then the school was moved into Clarksville, and an announcement appeared in the local newspaper in January, 1847, of the new name: The Clarksville Female Academy.

In spite of all their troubles, the faculty of two had the satisfaction that their students received the following tribute from editor Charles De Morse: "The graduating exercises of The Clarksville Female Academy drew many strangers to the place despite the mud underfoot. The recitations were full and perfect, the music enchanting, and the exhibitions of painting and wax work in the highest degree creditable to faculty and pupils alike . . . Success to the cause of female education!"

After another year, however, the success was still a financial failure, and the Weatherreds had to move to what was then called Titus County.

But the seed had been sown. The young ladies knew about Juliet and were ready for Romeo.

5.

Confederate Reunions

I n August the oldtimers of Red River County do more than watch the thermometers soar into the upper nineties and above the hundred-degree mark. They remember the gala time when the climax of summer meant only a light heart, a full stomach, blood tingling with the excitement of a very special emotion: the Confederate Reunions.

For a number of years after the War Between the States, the survivors who had worn the gray were so bitter that there was no place for any nostalgia. But in time a veterans' organization was inevitable, and in Clarksville a camp was established in the summer of 1890. The 306 charter members chose the name of John C. Burks Camp in honor of a young local lawyer who had risen to the rank of colonel and led his regiment to a hero's death at the Battle of Murfreesboro in Tennessee.

Ten acres northeast of Clarksville were purchased as a proper site for the annual get-together of the ex-Confederates and their families, and it was soon evident that a one-day affair was inadequate. Four and sometimes five days were

Confederate veterans at a reunion pose for a photograph.

needed for the former Rebels to enjoy themselves and one another.

Attendance grew from five to ten thousand. A dance pavilion, speaker's platform, and bandstand were erected, a well was dug, big tables were placed throughout the camping grounds, and finally a structure was built at the northeast corner for "Ladies" and one at the northwest for "Gentlemen." On a ten-acre campground one had to have a sense of direction and proper timing.

Dinners were all-out feasts with hundreds of pounds of barbecued beef, pork, and mutton "on the house." In addition, the ladies fried innumerable chickens, brought country hams, stirred up washtub-size bowls of potato salad, baked biscuits, and put out their prize jars of preserves and jelly. But when it came to the pies and cakes the battle lines were really drawn. There was no defense against the special favorite: the overwhelming strategy of piling three or four apple pies on top of each other and then cutting through them in thick slices like a layer cake. If that reinforcement could have been brought up before Richmond or Atlanta, neither Grant nor Sherman would have had a chance.

Coffee and lemonade were the usual beverages, although later on soda pop gained some favor. Naturally, whiskey was not absent, and since old whiskey barrels were used to hold the fresh well water, there was always a lingering flavor distinctive to the water. Each barrel had six tin cups tied on to it, and nobody gave a thought to germs or bacteria any more than they did to calories at the dinner tables. Of course, since most of the men wore beards and handlebar mustaches that retained varying amounts of tobacco juice or snuff, there was also some addition of this to the tasty water.

Highlighting the entertainment were the band music and the speeches. The Confederate reunions were the best captive audience any politician could have, and as their oratory ignited the regional patriotism in explaining why the War had been lost, few were left doubting if it had been lost at all. The steady flow of verbal fire wiped out any sense of defeat.

Whatever the words did not do, the music did, as the band swung out into "Tenting on the Old Camp Ground," "Maryland, My Maryland," "Bonnie Blue Flag," and over and over again "Dixie," which set off an explosion of rebel yells for at least quarter-hour periods without fail.

Only rarely was "The Star Spangled Banner" played, and when it was, nobody rose. Nor was it sung, for very few even knew the words.

The speakers were equally careful not to quote from Abraham Lincoln. To have done so was a good way to lose friends and votes.

However, the reunion in August of 1898 was different. The Spanish-American War was on, and men from the South and North were in the fight together now. Notably, the flags decorating the grounds were more Stars and Stripes than Stars and Bars. Banners were up reading "Remember the Maine, To Hell With Spain," and whenever the band played "Dixie" or "There'll Be A Hot Time in the Old Town Tonight," they also played "The Star Spangled Banner."

Later years brought carnival companies for the reunions, and a favorite with the Red River men was one called "The Forty-Nine Show." This featured girls who would dance with them for ten cents. The only trouble was that the veterans who found this attractive were too old to take full advantage of it. Even so, there were some who found that they could always get along without a crutch or cane at reunion time.

Gradually, too, as ice became more available, there were cold drink and ice cream stands around the grounds. Always the ice cream had been homemade and hand-turned. Now the factory product was on the market, and a couple of enterprising young fellows saw a potential fortune in the reunion appetite. They ordered twenty-five gallons to be shipped to Clarksville.

It arrived the night before the reunion, and the ice packing was melting under the August moon. Desperately they tried to repack it, but the damage was done, for the factory pack was one-fourth air. They lost over six gallons of ice cream before they could sell one cone.

Next day they worked like mad selling what they had. But the figures were plain. They had lost $8.46. In later years one of those boys became a Texas banker and the other a very successful Chicago manufacturer. Each claimed that he had learned his lesson early: not to engage in any business he did not understand.

When the automobile made its appearance, another couple of young men alert to opportunity brought one to the Clarksville Confederate Reunion and sold rides from town out to the camp grounds. Among those who dared to invest in the new transportation experience was a rather large colored woman who confided to her mistress that "I never really let my weight down in that thing."

After the Texas Baseball League was formed, a major attraction offered at the reunion was a three-game series between the Dallas and Waco teams. The guarantee was $500 a game, a good sum to the teams then.

But in one of the games a real crisis occurred when a New York player at centerfield for Waco suddenly called time and ran off the field in obviously great fright. At once the umpires dashed out to investigate. They found a horned toad, and until the little specimen of wildlife was removed, the athlete from Manhattan was in no condition to resume the game.

The toll of time finally rang down the curtain on the reunions of the Confederates in Red River County. After 1919 no more were held. But the stories were passed on from hand to eye and from lips to ear while new veterans of other wars came together.

6.

Red River Medicine

IN the days of the Republic of Texas and for a good many years afterwards almost any man could hang out his shingle announcing that he was a doctor. Only rarely were these claims challenged.

The public accepted such men as being what they said they were. Actually, most of them proved legitimate and many were highly skilled. Others were like the doctor on that southwestern frontier of America who used only two remedies: calomel for a purgative, and if an emetic was indicated, he caught a fly and gave it to his patient.

There were two schools of medicine. One was called the Botanic System and the other was termed Regular Practice. Some of the physicians used both methods just to play it safe.

There was a bit of legality involved in licensing doctors, but no more than in getting a hunting or fishing license today. No examination was required and there was no medical association. Nothing protected the public from quacks, and no consideration of professional ethics protected one doctor from another doctor's slander as a popular form of competition.

Some very interesting cases, both legal and medical, resulted from this situation.

One as early on the records as November 1839 began when a Red River County plantation owner by the name of Ed Hughart was feeling very ill. He had been "dragging" for several days, so he finally hitched up his horse and drove into Clarksville.

There on the public square he saw a sign on a window over one of the saloons: *John Davis, Physician.*

He went up and Dr. Davis felt his pulse, looked at his tongue, and mixed some medicine for him.

Hughart returned several times for more medicine, decided it was not doing him any good and stopped his visits. Then Dr. Davis billed him for $40, and, not having any ready cash, Hughart gave him a note. The doctor sued for payment of the note and won a judgment for $43.66⅔, which represented the principal, interest, and court costs.

Hughart got a lawyer and appealed the case. He did more than that. He accused Davis of not having a doctor's license in the first place.

Davis could not pay his lawyer, and he had "misplaced" his license. He rode away to bigger opportunities. Case dismissed.

*   *   *

On a February day in 1854 Dr. Ambrose Ellett sat in his office in Clarksville, definitely sick.

His office was empty. No patients, and that was what was the matter with him. Financial trouble was inducing a very bad nervous condition. There was entirely too much competition in this Red River town—ten doctors for about 750 population.

Suddenly fate knocked at his door. Not a patient, but a traveling salesman, Baldwin Judson, representing Comstock Bros. of New York, a drug company. Mr. Judson had a very attractive proposition to offer, for it seemed that his company was not at all satisfied with the local drugstore, Rhine and McDonna, as a retail outlet. He was prepared to give the doctor an exclusive agency for Comstock products.

The prospect and potential of this extra source of revenue gave Dr. Ellett instant relief. He brought out his special emergency whiskey, and he and Judson discussed all details. Judson would inform Rhine and McDonna of the change. He would also place an advertisement announcement for Dr. Ellett in the local paper, *The Northern Standard.* Meanwhile Ellett was to send his written order to Comstock for a shipment of merchandise.

In a flourishing hand he wrote:

February 24, 1854
Clarksville, Texas

Messrs. Comstock and Brother,
Please send me an assortment of your most saleable medicine to the amount of say One Hundred and Fifty Dollars worth at one half the retail price on twelve months credit with the privilege of exchange. Do not send any hair dye or vermifuge. Send a large lot of Almanacs with my advertisement on them, gratis.
A. K. Ellett, M.D.
Care E. Smith & Co.
New Orleans, Louisiana
Care Anne Monkhouse
Roland Red River, Texas.

While pleasantly engaged in this vision of future profits, he was unaware that Judson had visited Rhine and McDonna and received such a big order that they were allowed to retain the account.

And so two orders for drugs went to the Comstock Company, but as luck would have it, Rhine and McDonna's got to New York first and was shipped first.

Dr. Ellett's order was filled and sent on the next boat bound for New Orleans in April, the *Sultana* of the Holmes Lines.

From Comstock, whose invoice bore the address, "No. 2

Peter's Place, One door from Barclay Street (rear of Astor House)," five cases arrived, the contents of which included the newest drugs and medicine on the market. Among them were Judson's Cherry and Lungwort, Azor's Turkish Balm, Lee's Plasters, Acoustic Oil, Carlton's Pile Liniment and Heave Powders, Dr. Larzetti's June Cordial, Anti-Bilious Pills, Turkish Wine, Tooth Drops, Pain Killer, Pain Extract, Honduras Sarsaparilla, Eye Water, Hair Oil. The total came to $191.75 plus 3½ % insurance.

In June Dr. Ellett received notice from Rowland (or Roland) that the steamship *Echo* had arrived at the Red River port from New Orleans with five cases of goods for him. He hired a wagon and drove to get them, paying $40 freight charge.

Back again in Clarksville, he unloaded his cargo at his office and waited for business. But despite the announcement in *The Northern Standard,* business was anything but brisk.

On his way home that evening the doctor stopped by Rhine and McDonna's. It was no little shock to see a big new display of Comstock Almanacs and the shelves filled with all the latest remedies such as he had just received. Obviously, he was not an exclusive agent.

Rushing back to the office, he wrote his fury into a letter to Comstock telling them that they could have their merchandise when they paid him for the freight charges. They could never repay his distress and disgust.

Letters becoming more and more unpleasant went back and forth between Clarksville and New York until finally Comstock began a lawsuit against Dr. Ellett.

Expecting this, he had engaged a lawyer, J. A. N. Murray, who assured him that there was no cause for worry, thanks to a book which was becoming more and more popular every day as one person passed it on to another. The title was *Uncle Tom's Cabin.*

The doctor borrowed a copy from the lawyer and sat up all

night reading it. Then he understood why there was so much talk lately against "the North."

When the *Comstock vs. Ellett* case was called for trial in March, 1856, lawyer Murray saw to it that all members of the jury selected had read *Uncle Tom's Cabin*. No verdict was possible in favor of any "damyankee."

The jury recessed so briefly that they almost met themselves returning as they walked out.

The Comstock lawyers went home in defeat to read *Uncle Tom's Cabin*.

*   *   *

One of the best pieces of Red River folklore has always been the story of the man who traded a thousand acres of the richest blackland for a thousand boxes of malaria fever pills.

The old legend became historical fact recently when the files of the District Court of Red River County turned up Case No. 2039, the lawsuit of *Meredith Miles Marmaduke vs. William Becknell and Thomas J. Shannon*. The case was tried in December 1854, but the story of it began in 1838 and involved two very famous men, the governor of Missouri and "The Father of the Santa Fe Trail."

Meredith Marmaduke was born in Westmoreland County, Virginia, in 1791. During the War of 1812 he served as a regiment commander. In 1823 he went to Missouri and there he met Captain William Becknell, another ex-Virginian, who had led the first expedition from Independence west to Santa Fe just two years before. The trail was blazed now, and Becknell was the man of the hour. On his return trip he had brought jacks and jennets which became the founding stock of Missouri mules. At Becknell's invitation, Marmaduke joined him and made several very successful trading trips over the new route by wagon train.

The profits from such trips were as great as the dangers. In the first twenty years over $3,000,000 worth of goods was transported and sold, and some 3,000 wagons and 9,000 men were engaged in the business.

Marmaduke invested his money in a large farm in Saline County, Missouri. Finally finding time for romance, he fell in love with the daughter of the prominent Dr. John Sappington, who had made a fortune with fever pills for malaria. These pills, which were Missourians' most trusted medicine, contained quinine, dogwood bark, root, gum myrrh, licorice, and whiskey.

After his marriage to Miss Sappington, Marmaduke went into politics and was elected lieutenant governor in 1840. Four years later when Governor Reynolds died, Marmaduke became governor of Missouri.

Meanwhile Captain Becknell had not been resting on his laurels either. In the fall of 1835 he had led a band of Missouri men into northeastern Texas to engage in the revolution against Mexico. He called his company of mounted recruits The Red River Blues, and in the summer of 1836 they rode into south Texas, rifles cocked and ready to blaze away.

After the treaty at San Jacinto, Becknell came back to Red River County and settled there, some six miles west of Clarksville. He had been given a headright (veteran's reward) of 3,536 acres.

And so when Dr. Sappington came to Clarksville in 1838, he visited Captain Becknell, his old friend as well as his son-in-law's friend. This was when the famous trade took place, as Becknell gave the doctor his note for $2,000 in exchange for a thousand boxes of Sappington's Pills. Land, however good, was no good if you had malaria all the time.

On his return home to Missouri, Dr. Sappington gave the note to his son-in-law, and in 1844 Marmaduke sent the note to his resident agent in Texas, Tom Shannon, for settlement. He also appointed Shannon his trustee, because as a citizen of the United States and therefore an alien, Marmaduke could not hold title to land in the Republic of Texas.

Shannon, unfortunately, could not resist temptation and betrayed this trust, for when Becknell settled the note by deeding over a thousand acres of his land, Shannon did not report it to Governor Marmaduke.

Instead he sold the land to his brother James Shannon.

In due time, of course, Marmaduke learned what had happened and brought suit against his former agent for fraud. By the time he won it in the Supreme Court of Texas in 1855, both he and Becknell agreed that never had pills proved of such monetary, if not medical, value.

7.

City With No Mosquitoes

FROM the many references to the ravages of malaria in the Red River Valley, the theory of some regional historians is that this was the reason why the frontier towns which developed there never grew into major cities of any metropolitan size.

In the 1840's when Clarksville was booming with pioneer population, Dallas and Fort Worth did not even exist as names on any map. But as the years went by into the later decades of the nineteenth century, the population shifted and left the frontier behind. Better and more healthful locations beckoned, especially after other forms of transportation replaced the horse and steamboat.

After reading dozens of letters and diaries with descriptions of endless attacks of chills and fever, it becomes obvious that these early settlers faced a danger against which no rifle bullets could protect them. Nor could they know that thousands of miles away in another world an English doctor was at work researching an all-important theory about this danger, despite the ridicule of his superiors. In fact, at one time Dr. Ronald

Ross reached the limit of patience and said bitterly, "The man who can do is not allowed to do because the man who cannot do is put in authority over him."

But at last in the summer of 1898 he was able to announce the proof of this theory: the Anopheles mosquito bite was the cause of malaria.

The word of this discovery, so important to mankind that it was to bring Dr. Ross the Nobel Prize and knighthood, reached Red River County, and there another man began a campaign for public health.

He was Dr. Nowlin Watson, a veteran of the Spanish-American War of 1898 and a leading physician in Clarksville. He had studied the destructive effects of malaria in the army camps and at home. Armed now with the Ross discovery, Dr. Watson went into action. He knew that every house in the Clarksville area had open cisterns and that many people kept water which drained off the roofs into barrels, using it during the long summer dry spells. In these cisterns and barrels and in the two creeks which ran through the town, millions of "wiggle-tails" were bred which grew into mosquitoes and flew off to bite whatever was flesh and blood.

Until after the turn of the century very few houses were screened and not many persons had mosquito net bars over their beds. Some chemical repellents such as Pennyroyal were used, but in most cases black gunpowder, sulphur, rags, and sticks of punk were burned to drive off the swarms of insects.

Dr. Watson called a mass meeting of citizens at the city hall. With vivid accuracy he launched into this campaign against "the chill, with its paralyzed shivering, the chattering of teeth, the gooseflesh, the burning fever and headache, the intense thirst followed by drenching sweat, the enlargement of the spleen, and in severe attacks the emaciation, severe anemia, and great physical weakness and depression."

By the time Dr. Watson finished speaking and explained the mosquito bite as the cause, committees were formed and everybody went to work. Hundreds of wells and cisterns were covered, the creeks were oiled, collections of garbage were cleaned out, and whenever and wherever there was stagnant water, it was drained off.

Then Dr. Watson urged the simple building of "bat roosts," for he learned that bats feed on mosquitoes and naturally rid any place of them in record time.

Another expert who was called in suggested putting the small fish known as "gambusia" into the creeks because of their appetite for wiggle-tails.

The all-out campaign began to assume considerable cost, but this expense was met by public subscription. Among the contributions was a donation from the county, and when the commissioner who had arranged this was up for reelection, his opponent made an issue of it. He accused the commissioner of wasting public funds.

The commissioner promptly invited Dr. Watson to speak at the political meeting at the courthouse. At once the doctor began delivering his favorite speech on malaria, but only halfway through he had to stop. The new candidate had left the room and was prostrate with chills and fever and in urgent need of medical attention. He was through with politics.

Mosquito control had to be the work of not one but many years. The campaign expense became part of the Clarksville city budget, and the project is still conducted annually.

As soon as anyone in Clarksville sees a mosquito, that person calls city hall and gives the alarm. At once the central committee is alerted, and an extermination crew is sent out on patrol with all the latest equipment.

Cities many times larger have reason to envy this small town's chamber of commerce for its official letterhead, "The City With No Mosquitoes."

8.

Fairest of the Prairie Flowers

Among the earliest settlers in Red River County in 1835 was the Benjamin F. Brewster family who were descended from Elder Brewster, a passenger on the *Mayflower* voyage and a signer of the Mayflower Compact.

Ben Brewster had moved from Massachusetts to Connecticut and then to an island in the Allegheny River in Pennsylvania. Still he heard the call of new country and came to Texas, settling a few miles southwest of Clarksville on land which to this day is referred to as Brewster's Prairie. With him he brought his son and widowed daughter and her children, notably the eighteen-year-old pride of her grandfather's heart, Caroline Eleanor Cullum.

From every account, Caroline was a beauty with "gray eyes, brown hair, broad forehead, very positive mouth and lips, and always a complexion unmatched by others who have traveled the cow trails of Texas."

Every eligible young man in Clarksville was at her feet, only half-listening as she talked of poetry and music. Most especially did two young lawyers, Captain David Sample and Hiram Baker, devote themselves to her.

Finally in 1838 she made her choice between the two friends and married Captain Sample. Barely a year later President Mirabeau B. Lamar appointed Sample to act for the Republic of Texas in a survey to establish the boundary line between Texas and "The United States of the North."

Before leaving for the Sabine River to begin his work, Sample bought a horse from the minister who had so recently performed his marriage ceremony. But as he rode eastward on his new mount, Sample discovered that the clergyman had lied about the animal which could hardly make the trip.

Disillusioned with the minister and thoroughly disgusted, Captain Sample wrote a letter to the Secretary of the Treasury of the Republic of Texas, reporting the trickery and stopping payment on the note and draft for $200 to the Rev. Matthews. (Treasury Letters, Vol. I, pp. 286-7.)

Then after a letter of more tender style to Caroline, he bought another horse and proceeded with his project. But it was to be even more ill-fated for David Sample, for as he continued the survey along the Sabine, he became seriously ill and returned home to die in the arms of the wife he called "the very fairest of the prairie flowers."

His good friend and former rival, Hiram Baker, was appointed administrator of his estate. After several months he could contain himself no longer and wrote to Caroline:

Dear Lady:
Think not the disclosure premature when I own your modest worth has moved my heart, or my suit hasty in soliciting an interview with the lovely Mrs. Sample.

You will please answer me either verbally or by note as you may think most expedient.

If I am favored, in relation to time and place, you will act at your pleasure.

Believe my motives most honorable and sincere.

                              Yours in constancy.

In a few days his suspense was answered with this proper protest:

Dear Sir:

The contents of the billet surprise me very much, for to reciprocate your wishes would be perfectly out of my power at present. I consider myself highly honored by your good opinion. I am warmly attached to my friends, but no softer position can at present (I think) penetrate my cold and lacerated heart. I once pressed to my bosom one who possessed the most manly virtues and fewest faults. Still he was mortal. When my pillow is wet with tears for him, I cannot receive the addresses of another. Time and youth may effect much, more perhaps than I am aware of.

I would wish to retain your warmest friendship and forget that you have addressed me in any other language. Consider me a sister.

With due respect, your sincere friend.

It was not a letter to discourage Hiram Baker in any way—quite the contrary. His answer was immediate:

My Dear Caroline:

I am not so vain as to believe you anxious to have the note (enclosing this) intended as a duplicate of the original. My motive is to remind you of your partial promise of a requital, that I may be proud some future day to exhibit as an early specimen of your composition to our————. I beg your pardon, I had almost again incautiously committed the same mistake that suffused the check with such an interesting blush, so modest and so lovely. I am not romancing, for you know I love my 'dear Gazelle.'

Yours sincerely.

Caroline could not long resist capitulation, and with Victorian flair replied with this letter:

Dear Sir:

Do not believe me weak or fickleminded when I assure you it is with far different feelings I address you from what I had when writing the original of the note enclosing this. Think not that it has been flattery that has caused the change or that I have or ever can forget the object I once so dearly loved. Yet I feel (and very sensibly too) that you are fast taking his place in my heart and I look forward with greatest pleasure to brighter and happier days unless

Now too the joy most like divine
Of all I ever dreamed or knew,
To see thee, hear thee, call thee mine,
What misery should I lose that too.

Ah misery indeed, but I will banish such ideas from my mind and feast my imagination upon the belief that I possess one who is well aware how sincerely I am attached to him and that it is his many virtues alone that won my heart. What can come nearer real bliss, save possessing the object of so many agreeable reflections.

Believe me yours sincerely.

Very naturally, after this exchange of correspondence, more personal contact followed, and Caroline Sampler and Hiram Baker were married.

He continued his legal profession in Clarksville and also taught at the McKenzie Institute, the college of "classical education" which had been founded by a Methodist circuit-rider, John Witherspoon Pettigrew McKenzie.

The Bakers led a very happy life until the advent of the Civil War. Then his sympathy for Sam Houston's stand against secession made Baker so unpopular that he moved Caroline and their family to Wisconsin for the duration. Hiram Baker was at home in the north, for as early as 1837 he had held a teacher's certificate in Chicago. But after the war was over, the Bakers returned to Texas.

Again Caroline Cullum Sample Baker became a widow, and again her beauty, charm, and personality attracted a third husband, C. E. Cary, a retired lawyer from Vermont who had come to Texas.

She lived to be ninety years old, and only a short time before her death in 1906 in Weatherford, she gave an interview to the local newspaper, recalling vividly the days when men going off to the war between Texas and Mexico had stopped at her mother's house for coffee—and stopped again on their victorious return, fewer in number but still vowing that nowhere else was there such coffee between the Red and the Rio.

She was still too modest to acknowledge that the sight of a beautiful daugther might have added to the fame of her mother's coffeepot.

9.

O Tempora, O Mores

FOR a good many centuries man's afterthought on almost any problem affecting society has been, "There ought to be a law against . . ."

As a result, the total content of today's law school library is beyond any man's possible knowledge. We collect laws more avidly than any other single thing, and we seldom let go of them even after the changes of time and custom remove their application, fortunately or unfortunately, for enforcement.

For example, when the Congress of the Republic of Texas adopted a resolution incorporating the town of Clarksville in Red River County on December 29, 1837, the first laws passed and never repealed included the following:

The rate of taxation shall never exceed one percent. No single sentence in the literature of American history offers more beauty of nostalgia than this. Any further commentary would be to desecrate a design of words so perfect that a writer can only sit in awe of them, as in a museum. We submit it as a superb standard for all students of composition, if not economics.

Any person who shall appear in a public place in this city in a dress not belonging to his or her sex shall be deemed guilty of a misdemeanor and on conviction shall be fined not more than one hundred dollars. After reading this law still on the books as it was passed by a city council in solemn conclave, we can barely resist computing the yield in fines in our generation on the girls' and boys' attire.

Much the same thought comes to mind with this next law: *Any female who shall be found loitering upon the public streets unattended by male escort at a later hour than 10:00 o'clock P.M. upon conviction thereof shall be fined not exceeding ten dollars.*

The modern American woman smiles at such a legal antiquity of curfew and morals. However, it can become less remote, as it recently did to the East Texas schoolteacher who took her vacation in a Latin American country where a similar law still exists.

Happily strolling the streets in typical tourist fashion one evening, she was suddenly arrested as a streetwalker and taken to jail. The officer in charge, finding that she had five hundred dollars in traveler's checks in her pocketbook, informed her that this amount just happened to be the fine for not possessing a prostitute's license.

Before signing them over in frantic tears, she called the American embassy, but to no avail. It was a weekend and the persons of authority were weekending and could not be reached except in case of a national emergency. A Texas schoolteacher in jail did not consitute a national emergency.

In more tearful desperation she called the British consulate. At least they could speak English too. They not only could, but did. However, the gentleman in charge explained that he could do nothing officially for anyone not a citizen of Her Majesty's government. But as a man of experience like himself, he could personally make a very simple suggestion in solving her interesting crisis: Why not purchase a streetwalker's license? It only cost $2.50.

Gratefully she did so and was free to enjoy the rest of her nocturnal sightseeing. She returned home and proudly framed her certificate, no doubt the only schoolteacher in Texas with a license for professional streetwalking.

Another law of old Red River days in Clarksville is: *It shall be unlawful for anyone running a bar-room to permit any music to be made upon any instrument of any kind.* The same ordinance was also written to apply to any "house of ill fame," and in such a house it was also forbidden to permit dancing.

Obviously the city fathers on this frontier were men of a rather literal and single-minded approach to their drinking and sex life. If one went to a bar, it was to drink. If one went to a house of prostitution, why waste time? Perhaps this frustrated the development of the musical and dancing arts, but there may also have been some foresight of the unborn terrorist who would invent the jukebox.

It shall be unlawful for any automobile on a public street in the city of Clarksville to run for a greater speed than 8 miles per hour in the fire limits and over 15 miles per hour otherwise. No corner shall be turned at a greater speed than 8 miles per hour. In later years after the turn of the century when this law was added, their foresight was evidently slipping. So were the brakes to mechanical progress in the mad rush to be first to reach the red light.

Ignorantia legis neminem excusat.

10.

Ring Up the Curtain

BEFORE 1876 when the railroad chugged in and there was gradual improvement of wagon roads, public entertainment on the south shore of the Red River consisted of county fairs, fish fries, bridge raisings, baptizings, and public speaking on politics and religion—the more controversial the better.

The Red River County Fair featured not only horse racing but also another special attraction stemming directly from the romantic novels of Sir Walter Scott. The tournament at Ashby in *Ivanhoe* had its own variation and adaptation on this American frontier, as the young Texans rode the best horses they could train. Armed with lances, they galloped toward rings suspended above the ground, and whoever had the skill of getting the most rings on his lance had the privilege of crowning the young lady of his choice "The Queen of Love and Beauty." No honor was more coveted and prized, and it was a sad day for chivalry and romance in the Southwest when men were put into machines and could tilt only at stop signs.

After the Texas and Pacific Railway was completed in this region, traveling shows entered the scene, pitched their tents, and set a new stage and style of entertainment. No better treasury of personal report and cryptic commentary is available than in these excerpts from the private diary of W. M. Bowers:

October 27, 1874. The Fair came off on Tuesday, the last day of Court. A poor thing it was.

October 5, 1876. Howes Circus.

October 7, 1876. Fair commenced. Charles Dickson won the prize as ugliest boy. George Thompson cried because he did not win. Said he knew he was uglier.

May 5, 1877. Brick Pomeroy spoke on the greenback question. Cole's big show with a sea lion on Saturday.

April 10, 1880. Judson Hole preaching at Presbyterian Church. People going crazy over the singer.

November 8, 1881. Went to Paris (Texas) to see Barnum's big show. A smashing bobtail show at Reeves old elm tree near railroad on Wednesday. Cost 50¢ for whites, 10¢ negroes.

September 23, 1882. Inter-Ocean show here Saturday. Had a double-headed woman and 3 little twins.

March 24, 1884. Uncle Tom's Cabin show.

June 13, 1884. Bobtail show traveling on wagons was here. Would not send up their balloon because people would not give the man $5.00. A stinking liar.

October 9, 1884. Sells Bros. big show.

December 14, 1885. The Harry Leonak Theater showed here. The Farmer's Daughter.

January 24, 1886. Evangelist Peerson commenced a big protracted meeting at Presbyterian Church. Had over 100 converts. Some of Clarksville's hardest sinners.

April 3, 1888. A dime circus showed here Swiss bellringers and a woman with a big head.

July 6, 1889. Penn the evangelist preached at the big arbor. Had 135 new conversions and tightened the hoops on all the old ones.

March 8, 1890. Great balloon ascension of famous balloon man LeRoy. A perfect success. He lit in Bob Russell's farm west of town. The balloon beat him down.

April 28, 1890. Andrews Show sneaked by here. Failed to show as advertised. Fooled lots of people badly. Very good for us.

May 8, 1890. Evangelist Graves began 6 day meeting. We paid him $60.00.

November 8, 1890. Great election day. Grover Cleveland elected President and Adlai Ewing Stevenson Vice President. If the thieves don't steal it from them. [This referred to the Hayes-Tilden contest when many in the South thought that the election was stolen from Tilden the Democrat.]

November 12, 1892. Great torch light procession to celebrate Cleveland, Stevenson, and Hogg.

June 14, 1893. Sanders lectured here. No good.

October 14, 1893. Went to hear Sam Jones preach and a devil of a preach it was.

After 1893 very few of the tent shows came into the Red River region. This was not so much because of the financial panic in that year as it was the fact that a prosperous merchant by the name of N. D. Trilling built an opera house in Clarksville and better quality shows were attracted.

The Trilling Opera House replaced one which had been over a saloon (with an outside stairway, of course, to protect the ladies from contamination), where such classics as *East Lynne* and *Ten Nights in a Bar Room* had been presented with gusto if not artistry.

The Trilling opened with a gala performance starring Gladys Wallis (Mrs. Samuel Insull) and Joe Cawthorne. Later productions recalled by Harry Trilling (son of the owner), a former manager Charlie Gaines, and newspaperman Henry Goldberg included Lewis Morrison in *Faust,* Joseph Jefferson in *Rip Van Winkle,* the Primrose and Dockstader Minstrels, Nat Goodwin and Maxine Elliot (America's most beautiful woman) in *When We Were Twenty-One,* Creston Clark (a nephew of John Wilkes Booth) in *The Last of His Race, Peck's Bad Boy, Camille, Romeo and Juliet, The Fast Mail* (which always brought down the house), *Parsifal, For Her Sake, Looking For A Wife, Denver Express, Hello Bill, My Friend From Arkansas, The Clansman, Isle of Spice, Convict's Daughter, Gambler's Daughter, Minister's Son, Waifs of New York, The Cat and the Fiddle,* etc.

Obviously there was no lack of variety for the buggyloads of men and women who drove in from miles around. More and more settlers in the Indian Territory were also coming across the river. Theater business was almost as good as the long staple cotton which brought a ten-dollar premium per bale when shipped under a Clarksville bill of lading.

Nor did night life end with the theater. A former actor named C. S. Ruble formed a partnership with H. R. Riegler to open a Candy Kitchen and Oyster Parlor near the opera house. This was *the* place to go after the show to enjoy the specialty of an oyster loaf or quail on toast, topped off with fresh-made chocolate or the popular "ribbon" candy.

A colored man called "John the Rabbit" trapped the quail for Riegler and Ruble's, and the portion they served was two quail covered with a rich cream gravy. This cost fifty cents and was considered an expensive treat for a young man and his date.

Actually, if he entertained in this fashion often, it did put quite a dent in the pocket of a dry goods clerk making $45 a month or a prescription clerk at $60 a month. Bartenders made about $50, but their social life was definitely limited.

Across the railroad track and a half mile beyond Clarksville police jurisdiction was another facet of entertainment, the "house of the fancy women" as the veiled references termed it. There the slogan was simple as its patrons reported, "Treat, Trade, or Travel." The gentlemen were allowed a grace period of half an hour to make up their minds. Evidently they made them up to treat or trade because this place was operating as late as 1915, many years after the opera house, saloons, and county fairs were memories.

There were times it seems when the patrons of one form of entertainment became detoured into another so that the situation got confused for them and everyone else. For example, a couple of Indian Territory citizens came across the river to Clarksville to market their cotton. They visited a saloon and heard there that a show would be given at the opera house that night. On their way to get tickets and attend, they stopped at two more saloons, and by the time they took their seats in the theater, both men were in highly unstable moods. The play, *East Lynne,* tore at their hearts. The villain was an excellent actor, and thoroughly warmed to his part. He mistreated the heroine with a gusto matched only by her flair for being mistreated.

Finally the gallants from Indian Territory could stand it no longer. They jumped on the stage to rescue the lady and beat up the villain. Fortunately the sheriff of Red River County and two of his deputies were in the audience. It took all of them to rescue the play.

Many of the road shows did not travel with full personnel for a complete cast. They filled in with local persons for extras, and both the glory and pay involved were highly prized. But sometimes it caused trouble. It certainly did when *Quo Vadis* was performed and several Clarksville fellows were to appear as Roman soldiers.

The manager dressed them in tunics and drilled them in standing around holding a shield and spear and flat sword. All went well until intermission, when they went out for a few drinks of whiskey. Then, in the next act when the Christian martyrs were being abused, the "Romans" decided that they were on the wrong side and began helping the martyrs; and when the climax came and Ursus was to strangle the bull and save the heroine, these fellows beat the bull with their spears and broadswords. Of course, the "bull" split apart and the two men inside emerged howling. Thus did the righteous triumph over the ghost of Nero on the Red River.

Before the turn of the century a local group of talented young Negroes put together a show called "The Eight Jolly Coons," which often equalled the professional minstrel companies. One evening, however, when their audience was over half white, they concluded with a new feature tableau announced as "Miss Liberty Enlightening the World."

In this admirably conceived number a girl of high yellow

color and strikingly Junoesque figure whose name was Florence Jones played the title role. As the curtain rose she was to be seen as the Statue of Liberty holding up the great lamp. But there was trouble with the curtain and it would not go up. The manager, named most appropriately Finis, got under the curtain and began pushing it up with sheer muscle power. After all, the show must go on.

It did. But not as planned, for Finis had accidentally caught hold of Miss Jones's skirt with the curtain and was raising them both at the same time. It was a show of Liberty which nobody forgot, especially Finis when she finally kicked him off the stage.

Another night when a visiting theater company was performing, a female impersonator stole the show. One young man in the audience was so smitten that he tried to make a date with "Francis." When he came to the hotel to call, he was invited up to a room and treated to the sight of his date stropping a big Wade and Butcher razor, smoking a black cigar before his shaving mirror, and laughing his handsome head off at the joke. The gentleman caller fled and was said to have doubted even his own sister for several weeks after this devastating experience.

Before Clarksville had a siren, a fire alarm was sounded by shooting off pistols or rifles. Inevitably, one night when a play was in progress at the opera house, a fire broke out several blocks away and City Marshall Louis Brown shot his pistol six times out in the street. It was at this moment that the script called for one of the actors to say, "What is that?"

At once a prominent citizen, known for his readiness to speak at any public opportunity for political effect, rose from his usual front row center seat and explained the entire operational system of the local fire department to the dumfounded cast. The play continued only after an extra intermission for a necessary round of drinks backstage.

As was noted in one diary, "Sometimes it was hard to tell where the best show was—on or off stage."

11.

When Carnegie Lost Money

ANDREW Carnegie was used to giving money to worthy causes, but he was not used to losing it in bad investments.

In 1902 he lost $10,000 in Clarksville, a town he knew only on the Texas map.

It all began when the ladies of the Clarksville New Century Club heard of the philanthropist's offer to build public libraries. They wrote him of Clarksville's need, and Mr. Carnegie agreed to donate $10,000 if the townspeople gave the land and contracted to supply $1,000 a year for library maintenance.

The New Century Club ladies already had a small circulating library of their own and agreed they would donate those books to the public library, including such favorites as *David Harum, When Knighthood Was in Flower, Trilby,* and a translation of *Sappho.* Into each copy was pasted the following notice:

No. . . . .   Value. . . . .
CIRCULATING LIBRARY
Patrons of this Library agree to the following
Terms and Rules, being the contract between them
and
C. W. Walker:
1. Membership to Library   1 year $4.00
    "   "   6 months 2.50
    "   "   3 months 1.50
2. A single book 25 cents.
3. Persons taking out a book must deposit the
   value thereof.
4. Persons losing or injuring books must pay the
   full value for same (books).
5. Five cents must be paid for tearing a cover.
6. Books must be returned or re-entered at the
   end of two weeks, or a fine of 5 cts. for each
   day over that time will be charged, and if kept
   out over two months, the price for same must be
   paid in addition to the accrued rent and fines.

The "immoral" reputation of the Daudet novel *Sappho* had
reached even the Red River country, well advertised by news
of the arrest in New York of actress Olga Nethersole for playing the part on stage where an actor carried her up a circular
stair to an imagined boudoir. Readers hoped to find the book
less imaginary and more specific in this climax.

These as well as other reading interests spurred Clarksville's
contributions to buy a lot for the library building and to hire
a librarian, a position avidly sought because it paid $50 a
month.

The library was built and a grand opening celebration
honored Andrew Carnegie and local culture.

Then came the foreshadowing of the 1907 panic, and the
city withdrew its financial support of the library. The door
was closed. But, unfortunately, the door was not locked.

Gradually nocturnal visitors made off with the books. Then
the furniture. Boys' marksmanship came to be tested by their
ability to aim rocks through the windows. What was left of

the windows likewise became targets for Saturday night bottles thrown by those who had emptied them.

When a stranger came into town with a large family and saw the vacant, naturally air-conditioned building, he moved in. When cold weather blew in, he moved out.

Finally someone wrote Mr. Carnegie and reported what had happened to his public library building. In reply a Carnegie secretary wrote the New Century Club members that they were responsible.

Frantically the ladies flew to their husbands, fathers, brothers. At once the Texans reassured them. According to Texas laws no woman was responsible for anything.

Infinitely relieved, the club did not bother to answer the Carnegie letter.

On November 18, 1912, the town sold the library building for $3500 to a Mr. Tucker who remodeled it into a home. After some fire damage later, he sold it to a Mr. Dorsey who turned it into a hotel.

For fifty-five years there was no library. Sappho never had to compete with Lady Chatterley nor any of her later counterparts, at least not along the Red River.

12.

Good For What Ails You

I N the early 1890's when the owners of New York's brown-
stone fronts were summer vacationing abroad at fashion-
able spas such as Baden-Baden, leaders in the Red River
region spent part of "fly time," as they called the long hot
months, at health resorts of no little fame of their own.

Those who could afford the $3.00-a-day rate American
plan went to the hotels at Eureka Springs in northern
Arkansas. Others went to Harkins Springs in the Indian
Territory, which the Indians called Alachi. But the trip there
was difficult by hack, wagon, or horseback and involved fer-
rying across a couple of rivers. Nor were any accommodations
there, only campgrounds and wild hogs.

By far the most popular place was Dalby Springs in Bowie
County, Texas. From Clarksville the train went thirty miles
east to DeKalb and then a hack line took the guests the remaining ten miles to the Springs.

At the station in DeKalb some of the local boys carried
on quite a lucrative business for some time by meeting the
trains and selling old whiskey bottles filled with Dalby water

to the drummers who were not getting off to go to the resort. The mineral water was the same color as good whiskey, and the trick was to tell the men that they were getting bourbon at half-price because it was tax-free. By the time the train pulled out and they opened their bargain and took a good swig, it was too late to do anything but throw the bottles out the window—for the boys to pick up again.

By 1895 Dalby had three hotels, several stores, and a dance pavilion. During the summer season it was necessary to have reservations well in advance. American plan rates at the hotels were $2.00 a day, and the bountiful meals featuring venison and squirrel were served family style at long tables. Plumbing arrangements remained on the primitive side, but one hotel had a bathhouse boasting the first full-length bathtub southwest of St. Louis.

Warren Dalby, who founded the townsite in 1839, had a number of children and among them a son who became judge of the 102nd District, the Honorable Norman Leonard Dalby. A letter written in his eighties from Texarkana holds vivid firsthand recollections:

There were two main springs, the original, known in 1895 as the Farrier, which was in the fifty acres of the ball park, dancing pavilion and Farrier Hotel. There were also large spaces with shade trees under which great numbers of people camped in tents, and the grass was kept down by their horses and mules . . . Outside the Farrier enclosure and up the spring branch some 150 or 200 yards was another spring, the Pirkey. From each of these springs flowed water the color of whiskey. There was no difference in taste, but the water from the Pirkey spring had a darker color. There was always some controversy as to which spring had the stronger water.

Up the prong of the branch from the Pirkey spring some 400 yards was the Booth spring whose water was clear as crystal and much cooler than the Farrier or Pirkey.

Every night there was a dance for the guests of the Pirkey and Farrier hotels. The pavilion was an open shed made of oak boards rived out of timber grown there. Wesley Cooper and Ralph Burns who lived at DeKalb were the musicians, also a man named Bell who could play a violin, harp and bass viol all at the same time.

One of the main attractions at the resort in the 1890's was Dr. Louis A. Sager, who was famous as a physician and surgeon. He kept an office in a residence near the Pirkey spring, and there was a constant stream of patients going there all summer and into the fall and winter. He put up all his own medicine with his name on the labels.

About 1895 a man came with a proposition to build a railroad from what was called Finley Switch on the Cotton Belt Railroad some 10 miles southeast of Dalby Springs to intersect the transcontinental line of the Texas and Pacific Railroad north of Dalby. His idea was to do the survey himself and employ all local men for the work. In return they would earn the unheard-of wage of a dollar a day and in time become conductors and engineers, firemen and roadmasters.

At once he assembled a crew of all the available youth and began cutting a right-of-way through a forest wilderness of hardwood timber without a single clearing. The fellows worked only with axes and one or two crosscut saws. After weeks of arduous labor and many survey errors they completed a wagon roadway. . . . The gentleman paid them off with checks and departed for the purpose of arranging for material to build the road. He never came back. However, in due course, his checks did. And the boys were left to look at their calloused hands and worthless checks.

Not to be outdone, they got a yoke of oxen and went down the public road to the gin where an old boiler had been thrown aside after its usefulness. With the oxen they pulled the old boiler into the road, pried it up with the dome upward, cribbed up under it to about the height of their heads and then took the cordwood from the gin and built a railroad around the gin toward the town of Bassett . . . The final wind-up of this effort for transportation was the prosecution of the boys for obstructing a public highway. So far as is known, that is the last ever done to get a railroad to Dalby Springs.

Another institution there during the early nineties was a Confederate Veterans Reunion for three days every summer. A man named Shaw came and introduced badger fights. These fights were carried on with a large wooden box which nobody could see into. Under this box was placed the "badger," really an old-fashioned chamber pot, sometimes called a "white owl." Through its handle was looped a trace chain, so that the person pulling the "badger" out would be "out of danger." After this was rigged up, a man claiming to be the owner of the vicious animal would challenge another man who had a fierce dog for a fight between the badger and dog. A crowd would gather around and a controversy inevitably arose between the men. They would come almost to blows and threaten each other with all kinds of physical violence as to which one would pull the badger out of the box in such a way as to give the advantage to badger or dog.

Some gentleman in the crowd would volunteer his services as a disinterested party in order to end the argument. When all this was arranged and the dog brought up close to the box, a master of ceremonies would yell, "All ready!" He would raise the box, call to the man with the chain to pull, and instead of a badger out would come rolling the chamber pot. Everybody would laugh and the victim of the joke would really be ready to fight. . . .

Dr. Sager died in 1898, and the decline of Dalby Springs began, until finally there were no hotels or boarding houses, only one store and the look of a rural ghost town. Now a state highway is less than a mile away, and the springs are still flowing with the mineral water in the same rustically scenic setting. Nature provides the spa potential which could just as readily attract another generation as it did before when, in the early 1880's, hotel proprietor J. W. Farrier had printed and distributed the following brochure:

The Dalby Springs are several in number, the Great Red Spring, the Salt Spring, Black and White Sulphur Wells, and the one known as the Headache Spring having gained the greatest celebrity.

These waters are powerfully tonic, diuretic and diaphoretic in character, and they have earned an unrivalled reputation for the cure of Dyspesia (in all forms), Dropsy (both local and general), Paralysis, Enlargement of the Spleen and Liver, Scrofula, Gravel, Constipation, Kidney and Genito-Urinary Diseases and all the diseases pecular to females. Delicate ladies and sickly children can resort to the waters with the assurance that health and vigor will be obtained. The cold, delicious, invigorating water of the Red Spring is a specific for Dsypepsia, there being *not a single case on record of failure to cure.*

The Hotel has been repaired and renovated, and a spacious, handsome addition completed. The house is filled with elegant new furniture, and guests will find everything clean and fresh.

Rooms large and airy. Not a mosquito to disturb the repose of the invalid or pleasure-seeker. The table is supplied with the best of everything, including wild game of all kinds. The surrounding country abounds in deer, squirrels, wild turkeys, ducks, etc., while the lake, three or four miles away, is full of fish. Facilities for Dancing (ball room separate from main building), Riding, Driving and other amusements provided.

All guests, especially invalids, will receive the untiring attention of the proprietor and his assistants. Persons from the North will find this a most delightful and beneficial winter resort, as the water is as beneficial in winter as in summer. Bath Houses are conveniently arranged . . .

After this introduction of attractions, Mr. Farrier listed sixteen testimonials from guests of prominence. For example:

The two weeks that I used the waters of Dalby Springs satisfied me of their great efficacy in kidney and bladder complaints . . .

J. W. Throckmorton
Ex-Governor of Texas, 1866-7

I had gravel of ten years standing and after remaining at Dalby three months I was entirely cured. The last month of my stay I gained thirty-six pounds.

J. G. Settlemyer
Knoxville, Tennessee

I went to Dalby Springs after trying other watering places, one of which was Hot Springs, Arkansas. I had my health restored at Dalby after suffering for months; was unable to stand when I went there and had to be hauled in a hack. I stayed six weeks and was entirely cured.
I have been sending my family there every summer for eight years and regard it as the best watering place in the South or Southwest for almost any disease.

S. D. Lary
County Judge, Bowie County

I have fully investigated the curative properties of Dalby water, having a kidney complaint that some of the best physicians in the State could not cure. I was so low when I started to Dalby that it was feared I would never reach there alive. I began to use the water and was entirely relieved in two weeks. Dalby saved my life.

Nettie L. Bennett

I have been a frequent visitor at Dalby Springs and have great confidence in the waters. They have repeatedly restored my little girl to health when all other remedies failed.

R. R. Gaines
Associate Justice,
Texas Supreme Court

Early in the summer of 1879 my little eighteen-month-old son was taken sick with Dysentery, then Flux and finally Cholera Infantum. After the physicians gave him up to die, my wife in despair decided to start with the little fellow to Dalby. We hardly hoped the child would live to reach the Springs. Upon our arrival he was put on the water at once and his stomach retained it, though it had rejected everything for some time . . . In three weeks he was restored to vigorous health and is a stout, healthy boy now in 1882. After commencing the water he took no medicine whatever. Dalby Springs saved my child's life. It is the most valuable water in the world.

O. F. Parrish

With the development and prosperity of Texas comes the fact that many who, after toiling industry and confinement to business, find it necessary to seek a place of rest and retreat; and from experience I believe the healing qualities of Dalby Springs deserve a name among those of the widest fame. I regard the water highly valuable in cases of stomach trouble and weak digestion. They are solvent and act finely on the Kidneys, thereby freeing the system of effete matter and benefit both male and female. Visitors will find the proprietor and his very estimable lady highly entertaining and agreeable.

S. E. Clement
President, Paris Exchange Bank

I have been acquainted with the great medicinal virtues of the water of Dalby Springs for upwards of twenty-five years and am satisfied that they have never been appreciated as they should be. They possess superior tonic properties (iron being one of the leading ingredients) and as a laxative, diaphoretic, diuretic and soporific they have no equal. If your constitution is broken down from disease or overwork, go to Dalby. If you or your children have contagious (skin) disease, go to Dalby. If you have any Kidney, Bladder, in fact any urinary disease, go to Dalby. If your nervous system is irritable and you cannot sleep well, go to Dalby. If your stomach is deranged from indigestion or any cause, be certain to go to Dalby. From my knowledge of the diseases of this country, after having practiced my profession for many years, I know of few diseases, if any, that will not be greatly benefitted by a stay of from ten to twenty days at Dalby. Were the best chemists of the U. S. to analyze these waters and then compound all of said ingredients for a patient, it would not have one-half the effect the waters will when taken fresh and sparkling from the springs. Nature's God is the best chemist and prescriptioner we have.

W. W. Stell, M. D

The list goes on with equal eloquence from mayors, clergy, and senators. Nor were any of the testimonials arranged for commercially. In fact, as one elderly gentleman states, "That would have been considered a personal insult and those men would have worn out their walking canes on you for even offering to pay for their testimony."

Dallas News columnist and author Frank X. Tolbert has reported an interview with one Andrew Dodge, 107 years old, of Bowie County, who attributed his prolonged health to the Black Springs water. "I've drunk from the Black Spring most of my life. Keeps me frolicky," Mr. Tolbert quoted from Mr. Dodge, plus the added information that "Uncle Andrew only recently gave up horseback riding and coon, possum, and fox hunts."

Another interview featured in the same column with Roy Dalby, a son of the original founder, described the Black Spring water as coffee-colored and stressed the fact that this water was never known to freeze, regardless of winter's lowest temperature readings.

The wonders of Dalby Springs never ceased. Only Dalby did.

13.

Christmas 1863

IT was anything but a merry Christmas Day for Rhoda Bowers and her children in their home in Clarksville in 1863,
for like thousands of other families all across the country they
knew no peace upon their earth and no good will.

Even in the Red River Valley the enemy they feared and
hated was little over a hundred miles away, the enemy that was
keeping their husband and father away from them.

What good is Christmas in wartime when men are fighting
and killing? Rhoda Bowers had no satisfactory answer for
young Martha and Eugene and Cloudy. All she could do was
to make them realize that however un-Christmasy it was for
them, it was much worse for their father wherever he was.
Besides, had they not the best of all reasons to celebrate? A
letter had come from him, delivered by a trusted friend. What
more could they ask for? There was hope, and hope was
Christmas.

Eagerly they begged to write a letter in return, a letter of
good cheer, a real Christmas letter. She agreed that this was
the very best thing they could do. But because of the scarcity
of paper they must write it all on a single sheet.

And so while a big pot of "coffee" made from okra seed was boiling, and by the light of tallow candles, they gathered around the table and wrote a letter which Will Bowers was to get and carry in his breastpocket under his Confederate Army coat and finally bring home from the war to paste in his diary, its ink still clear today after a century.

Clarksville, Texas
December 25, 1863

Dear Papa,

I seat myself to write you a few lines to let you know I am well at present hoping when these few lines reach you they may find you enjoying the same blessing. You don't know how proud it makes your boy to get a letter from his papa. It would make him still prouder to see you papa. I want you to make haste and bring me that powder flask and try to find me a little gun and then I will begin to think I am man enough to stand guard for you when you are away from home. I wish the old war would end so you could get to come home and stay with us for we miss you so much. I wish to God that you would get that little shot gun to go with my powder flask for I can't help from thinking about it. I expect I will be thinking about it all night. Now if I had it I would shoot a great big Christmas gun instead of shooting bladders[1] but you know papa all little boys must have their day. You must not think anybody wrote this letter but your boy Eugene. I caught some Christmas gifts and got an apple. Good night. Papa let me hear from you soon. So no more at present. I only remain your son until death.

Eugene M. Bowers

God shelter and protect you is the sincere prayer of your wife. I will close as the children want to write.

Rhoda H. Bowers

Dear Father,

I seat myself for the first time in life to write you to let you know that we are all well. We received your letters that you sent by Mr. Wilson which gave us all satisfaction. Pa I have been to preaching twice this Christmas but it seems that I will not get to go anymore

---

[1]This refers to the custom then of blowing up hog bladders and jumping on them. This holiday game was popular as late at 1900.

for it is pouring rain and has been all day. Pa I would feel more than proud if you were here with us setting by the fire instead of being out in the cold rain where I am afraid you are. Pa Ma wont go nowhere. She just stays at home and talks and thinks of you. I cant persuade her to go anywhere. She thinks if she goes away nothing will be done right at home. She says she has no heart to visit. So come home soon pa. Cloudy is out in the rain riding the banisters with your big whip hollering for Kit to come up. He lets on like they are about to run away with him. So no more at present but remain your true and affectionate daughter until death.

Martha F. Bowers

Dear Papa,

Your little Cloudy takes this opportunity to write you a few lines. I dont intend the rest of the children shall outdo. If they can write better than I can you know your little boy has great confidence in himself being a man. Papa you must bring me one present. Do not bring them all to Bud. A little pistol will do me. Papa you told me to tell you how my sow and pigs come along. They are all well and just as fat as butter balls. The little sow has the prettiest pigs you ever saw. So no more at present but I remain your youngest son until death.

Cloudy M. Bowers

There were happier Christmases for this family in later years but none more memorable, for their prayers were answered and Will Bowers was spared to return to them the next year.

The reference young Cloudy made to the sow and pigs being "fat as butter balls" indicates that the Bowers were more fortunate than many families at that time in their region. After Lincoln's Emancipation Proclamation, numbers of slaves left their masters and began drifting away. But a mulatto named Win whom Bowers had bought in 1854 for $1200 stayed with them devotedly and worked some land a couple of miles west of Clarksville, raising corn and wheat and a few hogs. While Bowers was away in the army, this crop enabled his wife to pay her taxes "in kind" in the way of supplies for the Confederate army instead of the valueless government currency.

In fact, even after Will Bowers returned home he still pasted in his diary such tax receipts as the following:

> Clarksville, Texas
> November 11th, 1864
> Received of W. M. Bowers 131
> Pounds of Bacon his taxes
> in Kind for 1864.
> W. N. Smith
> Agent Subsistence Dept.

After the war when Win finally agreed to accept his freedom, he took the name of Win Bowers. As a good carpenter he formed a partnership with his former master in the contracting business until he could establish himself as an independent contractor. When Win died he owned nearly a block of business buildings in Clarksville as well as other property. It was no little achievement for an ex-slave.

There was only one problem which even the Bowers family could not solve. At Win's funeral so many heirs presented themselves claiming to be his children that there was no way to tell who were and who were not.

But again Christmas was approaching, and so they all got together and agreed to an equal division among them. No estate was ever settled more simply, amiably, peacefully. After all, it was a Christmas gift, which was the way Win would have liked it.

William M. Bowers, grandfather
of co-author Eugene W. Bowers,
left a wry commentary on current events in his diary.

Amos Morrill, "The Mighty
Morrill," was a brilliant ruthless
lawyer who loved nothing beter
than a good legal fight. He lived
in Clarksville from 1839 to
1856 and eventually became
Federal Judge of the Eastern
District of Texas.

Amos Morrill.

14.

The Mighty Morrill

R EADING the source material of nineteenth-century history of the Southwest reveals one very obvious fact: law was the most important of all professions as soon as the land was settled. Legal conflict replaced military conflict. Instead of fighting, men sued for protection and justice.

Nowhere was this more in evidence than in Red River County where the laws of more than one nation were involved. For example, a planter by the name of James Ward engaged in so much litigation that he set some sort of record. From 1840 to 1859 he figured in one hundred and thirty-one lawsuits—as defendant one hundred and fourteen times, as plaintiff seventeen times. One wonders how he managed time to run his plantation.

Among the luminaries in the courts south of the Red River no name and no personality generated as much fame and sensational controversy as that of Amos Morrill. In many ways the man was a forerunner combination of Darrow-Rogers-Ernst-Nizer. None of his clients were ever in as much trouble as he was. Nor did any man ever enjoy a finer finale after seventy-four years of *Sturm und Drang*.

Amos Morrill was born in Salisbury, Massachusetts, on August 25, 1809. He graduated from Bowdoin College in the class of 1834 and began his first adventure by going into the wilds of Tennessee to teach school. After a year of that he returned home and "read law" in Salisbury with R. Cross, Esq. But again adventure called and he went to Murfreesboro, Tennessee, and into the law office of Henderson Yoakum, a West Point graduate of 1832.

From Yoakum, who later was to write the first important history of Texas[1] with Sam Houston's help, young Morrill began hearing about the new frontier to the west. In 1839 Morrill came to Clarksville where the pioneer challenge matched his ambition. There he married Miss M. A. Dickinson.

At once his brilliance attracted attention, coupled as it was with a fiery ruthlessness in dealing with any opposing lawyer. When Amos Morrill tried a case, it was a show that drew an audience. No holds were barred in his technique. But inevitably this method and manner were to backfire against him any number of times. In addition, Morrill remained a Whig in politics and never compromised in any way with Southern thought and feeling. Few men of prominence ever rose higher on the shoulders of more enemies. Yet so authentic was his knowledge and so fearless his courage that even those enemies were wary of any triumph over him, however temporary it might be.

A case in point was in 1841 when he was engaged by a Mr. Hamilton Lennox of Crawford County, Missouri, to collect a note payable to John Tweedy against James Ward. Lennox had bought the note from Tweedy, who failed to endorse and transfer it before he died.

When the suit was ready for trail, Ward paid Morrill a hundred dollars to continue the case. Then Ward reported

[1] Vol. II. *History of Texas From Its First Settlement 1685 to Annexation to United States 1846.* Facsimile Edition published by Steck-Vaughn Co., Austin, Texas.

this to Judge John T. Mills and filed a charge against Morrill for taking a bribe.

The judge immediately appointed a committee of the district attorney and four other lawyers to investigate the matter. Their report filed in early October 1842 verified the fact as stated by the vengeful Mr. Ward. Amos Morrill had accepted the hundred dollars, but in extenuation was his previous intention to have continued the case anyway as agreed with his client. Furthermore, Morrill was under agreement to pay all court costs if he failed in the case and was to receive as fee twenty percent of the note if he won the case for his client.

Judge Mills grimly delivered his opinion to the court more severely than anyone expected. After reviewing the details he minced no words in describing Amos Morrill's conduct as a discrace to the legal profession, the loss of honor as a gentleman, plus the offense of champerty as defined by Sir William Blackstone himself. In conclusion the judge also expressed "my utter contempt for the low agitator James J. Ward who by charge of offering a bribe has shown himself to be a dangerous man in society. *He who will give, will take a bribe* is a maxim in morals and never more true than in this instance . . . I feel it my duty to make these remarks because I believe that James J. Ward has exposed Mr. Morrill for the purpose of gratifying some petty private pique of his own and not from a sense of duty . . ."

Finally Judge Mills ordered a decree that Amos Morrill be suspended from practice in any court of the Republic of Texas.

Everyone was shocked as young Morrill saw his career ended. This concerned him more than any loss of reputation, for he knew that his exposure was only for what other attorneys did and would not admit.

Next day an appeal was made by a member of the investigating committee to the court to reconsider, and another committee was appointed. Five months later when the spring term of court convened, the committee's report recommending for Morrill's reinstatement was presented. Judge Mills accepted and acted upon it, rescinding his order, and again Amos Morrill was back in business.

Ringing in the ears of all the members of the bar at court was the old judge's warning "to let their walk be upright, let their acts be open, bold and determined, and the petty slanders which are retailed by the ignorant and vulgar against the professions will cease."

It had not been an easy winter for Amos Morrill. His temper had cooled down to boiling point, and he was acutely aware of the gratitude due the men who had signed that appeal for him.

Among those names was Charles DeMorse, editor and publisher of the *Northern Standard,* second oldest newspaper in Texas. Yet, in ten years' time these friends were to become enemies and oppose each other in the biggest ante-bellum libel suit on record.

"The Father of Texas Journalism" as he was often called, Charles DeMorse was also from Massachusetts, and at first this was always a bond between him and Amos Morrill.

As a boy DeMorse had moved with his family to New York, where he spent his school years and studied law while his father ran the Tontine Coffee House on Wall Street. The lawyer Van Wyck under whom young DeMorse studied was a brother-in-law of Samuel Maverick of Texas, and so there was much talk about the new country which was revolting against Mexican tyranny. When a "battalion" of emigrants was organized in New York in the fall of 1835 by Texas' Major Edwin Morehouse, DeMorse joined with 173 other volunteers who sailed out of New York harbor on the brig *Matawomkeag.*

They sailed into adventure long before reaching Texas, for in only three weeks a British warship forced them into Nassau as suspect pirates. After a month spent convincing the authorities there that they were only volunteer patriots, they set out again for Texas. Eventually, after a stop in New Orleans long enough to get into and out of a duel, DeMorse landed on Texas soil in early March, 1836. At once he set

out to find General Houston and his army, but instead he
met the officers of the new Texas Navy and joined them as
a marine lieutenant on the seven-gun schooner *Independence*.
After San Jacinto it was DeMorse who guarded Santa Anna
when the infamous prisoner was brought on board by the
Texas officials to sail from Galveston Island to Velasco.

Heady with all the excitement of the time and place, De-
Morse knew he must stay in Texas. He chose Matagorda and
began the practice of law. There too he married the daughter
of Colonel Thomas Wooldridge, first American consul at the
port as appointed by President Andrew Jackson.

In 1839 DeMorse and his family moved to the new capital
Austin, though it was still only wilderness. There he found his
real métier as editor-reporter for the House of Representatives.
Then the Red River District delegates to Congress urged him
to open a newspaper in Clarksville and offered to finance him.
In March 1842 he moved to Clarksville and on August 20
rolled his first issue off a George Washington hand press. For
forty-five years he was to continue to produce the paper that
reflected his own devotion to the ideals of journalism and
patriotism.

With his fellow New Englander, Amos Morrill, he differed
only on politics, for DeMorse was a staunch Democrat and
thoroughly Southern in sympathy. As a lawyer he had to ad-
mire Morrill's great talent. But some accident of circumstance
triggered the trouble between them.

To sit in the Old Red River County Courthouse and read
through the two big boxes of documents related to that trial
is to realize that the many men who were drawn into it and
who later left their mark on regional and national history
were all affected by the rising hysteria of strife which was
to tear not only them but a nation apart. Emotion is still
fresh in those papers of over a century ago, and in perspective
it is perhaps more evident then it was to them. But the battle
lines of tensions were forming between North and South in
Clarksville as they were elsewhere. In subtle ways this was

at the core of what seemed to be only personal in this trial.

Morrill's enemies had been biding their time since he had made his professional comeback. When a new lawyer John Summers came from Kentucky to begin practice in the spring of 1853, they assured him that he would make himself popular by filing a complaint against Morrill on charges of professional misconduct, so that this time he would be permanently removed from practice.

The newcomer scapegoat did as he was told, fondly believing that this would be a shortcut to fame and success. He charged Mr. Morrill with acts such as abandoning a client after taking her money and also taking out answers filed by a defendant so as to permit a plaintiff to take judgment by default, then returning the answers and causing judgment to be reversed.

When the full complaint was presented to Judge W. S. Todd, His Honor appointed a committee to investigate the charges. The committee reported that all the charges were false. This should have ended the matter, but Judge Todd saw fit to reprimand Mr. Morrill for arousing such suspicion. To Morrill this added insult to injury, and he made a reply which increased the temperature in the courtroom by several degrees.

His own temper flaring, the judge ordered him held in contempt of court and fined ten dollars. This too should have concluded the incident, but in the June 7, 1853 issue of *The Standard,* editor DeMorse published an account of what had happened in court that week.

The news item appeared on the front page with stories reporting Captain McClure's discovery of the Northwest Passage, Harriet Beecher Stowe's entertainment at Stafford House in London, the Pope's prohibition of circulation of *Uncle Tom's Cabin,* French preparation to oppose Russia, and Germany's imprisonment of Professor Gervinius as author of *Introduction to the History of the Nineteenth Century* and the burning of his "treasonable" book.

Morrill called in Judge G. A. Everts of Bonham to assist him in filing a suit against DeMorse for libel damages in the amount of $20,000.

The figure was fabulous in 1853, and the announcement whetted everybody's appetite for the fight ahead.

At once the editor engaged Judge John T. Mills to defend him. This was a situation which would have pleased even Mr. Pickwick, for the enmity of the opponents was matched only by that of the attorneys representing them. They all hated one other personally, so that the contest promised enough violence to shake the foundations of the new courthouse.

For three years the case was continued from term to term as each side gathered its ammunition. At last the trial opened on March 7, 1856. Dozens of witnesses had been called to supply evidence, and many—because of distance and travel difficulty—testified by sworn depositions which were read to the court.

The strong features of his handsome head tense but composed under a rigid discipline, his keen eyes watchful and perceptive of effect, Amos Morrill sat and heard the forty-seven years of his vigorous, aggressive life pass in review as the men he had known gave their varied opinions of him. Among them were his first partner in Tennessee, lawyer-historian Henderson Yoakum of Huntsville, Texas; J. Pinckney Henderson of San Augustine, Secretary of State and ambassador to France for the Republic of Texas, a major general in the war with Mexico, a law partner with General Thomas J. Rusk, a first governor of Texas after annexation to the United States.

There was also Frank Clark, son of the founder of Clarksville, who flatly stated that he had written the newspaper report about Morrill whose "reputation is the reverse of an honorable man." Then the first sheriff of Red River County, William C. Young, who was to become a Confederate Army general, expressed his "view as a Southerner" in reference

s to be a bridge-raising that would go down in the
ords of 1893 as just about the ultimate, for the
who were the hosts arranged to combine a fish
lic speaking, and a baptizing for their guests.

miles south of the new bridge was Turner's Lake,
seined that in order to get hundreds of pounds of
sh. When the guests arrived they could smell the
ng in four huge iron vats filled with boiling grease
pasture. Vast slabs of cornbread were cooking, a
barbecued, and seemingly endless kettles of coffee
ng between the long tables set up to accommodate

the most popular men in the region arrived with his
rish of personality. He was Uncle Charles Fowler.
lmost nattily groomed from his boots to his little
tee, he cut quite a figure as he called greetings
left. In fact, folks often wondered why and how
arles kept out of politics. With a high temper always
d ready for a fight or frolic, he was never in the
d where any audience assembled.

was no exception as he spied a stranger in the crowd,
r to him, and let go a good right to the man's jaw.
ody was delighted with the prospect of so much
t to spark the party. Here was a good fight to enjoy
nations could come later.

hile the stranger, who was said to be a book sales-
vered himself and returned the attack. He went into
vith Uncle Charles and managed to get a firm grip
wler goatee. Down they both went in what was called
at roll" which finally became so violent that they
pulled apart. By then half of Uncle Charles' goatee
and the stranger had a good part of his ear bitten
one agreed that it was as fine a "wool pulling" and
inning" as any professionals could have exhibited.
the principals were given first aid, Uncle Charles
that the peddler had been at his house the day before

to both Morrill and DeMorse as "Yankees," acknowledging rather grudgingly the editor as the lesser of two such evils in the community. He also firmly stated his refusal at one time to cooperate with Morrill in a suit to obtain the freedom of a Negro girl.

When at last all the evidence was heard, Judge Todd gave his fully detailed charge to the jury. In a remarkably short time they returned with their verdict which was in favor of Amos Morrill, but the amount was reduced from $20,000 to $8,000.

At once Morrill sprang to his feet, expressed his appreciation of their justice, and then with characteristic impulse of beau geste he remitted all the damages awarded, accepting only the payment for actual court costs.

It was over, and despite the prejudice against him, he had won and vindicated himself. It was no small triumph in his strife-torn career.

Later in the year he was charged in Lamar County with passing counterfeit money. He demanded a jury trial and again was acquitted. Still his enemies kept after him, and he was charged with perjury. Yet again he was tried and acquitted.

Morrill obviously recognized that it was time for him to move, and he did. He went to Austin and formed a law partnership with Andrew Jackson Hamilton, who was later to become governor of Texas and who shared Morrill's political thinking against secession.

In Austin the Morrills built a two-story stone mansion, above the north bank of the Colorado River, but their enjoyment of their new home was brief. The feeling about secession was making it unhealthy for any Unionist sympathizer. Civil war was upon the country.

Amos Morrill went to Mexico and then to Massachusetts. While he was in New England in 1864 his alma mater Bowdoin College conferred a Master of Arts degree upon him.

However, nothing could have been more indicative of Morrill's emotional ties than the fact that as soon as Union forces captured New Orleans he went there, and as soon as the war was over he returned to Austin. He had not believed in the Confederacy, but he believed in Texas.

When General Sheridan appointed E. M. Pease as Governor of Texas, Pease appointed Amos Morrill Chief Justice of the Supreme Court in 1868. Four years later President Grant appointed him Federal Judge of the Eastern District of Texas. As a jurist his record of decisions was memorable for the brilliance which had always attracted so much admiration and an equal measure of irritation. To him the law was thunder and lightning, and he rode the storm with a strange combination of dignity and delight.

There were persons who always wondered why an enemy did not kill him. It would seem that they feared his ghost would prosecute the case.

And so it was that in the seventy-fifth year of his life and in the setting he loved best, at home in Austin in view of the Capitol, Judge Morrill rested his case.

This w
social re
gentleme
fry, a pu

Severa
and the
fresh ca
fish coo
out in t
steer wa
were bo
the crow

One
usual fl
Neatly,
black g
right an
Uncle C
geared
backgro

Tod
strode

Ever
excitem
and ex

Mea
man, r
a clinc
on the
a "ton
had to
was go
off. E
"onion

Wh
explai

PERHAPS the most memorabl
relished by the Red River
events not usually listed in the en
most popular of these amusemen

At first while the land was bei
creeks were crossed by simply pu
beds and then trusting to luck tha
of wagon or carriage would not
But in time as settlement steadily
was levied for road and bridge b
came from the county and most of
benefit from such improvements i
farms, and businesses.

When a real bridge was buil
finished product to aid transportatic
with a ceremony and party. A go
which the Bowers family of three
when a bridge was built across L
miles south of Clarksville.

and forced his way in, trying to sell a copy of *Pilgrim's Progress*. This had annoyed Aunt Becky Fowler, and when Uncle Charles came in from the garden to rescue her from this hard-sell disciple of John Bunyan, he had to make a "razoo" at the fellow with a grubbing hoe to get rid of him.

Naturally, the sight of the offender here among a social gathering was a signal for action.

Now that the fight was over, they all had a fine appetite, and dinner was served in heaping platters and mugs. Brother Terry, the Baptist parson, was called upon to return thanks. He took out his Waterbury watch and prayed for ten minutes. After that it was every man, woman, and child for himself. Everybody ate too much, thoroughly relished it, and considered a spoon of soda afterwards a small price to pay for such a magnificent heartburn.

After dinner the program featured Captain Thomas, a lawyer with quite a reputation for oratory. As his admirers said, "He could really put the dew on the violets."

An ex-Confederate officer of course, Capt. Thomas was something of a rarity, because his military title was entirely bona fide and not a matter of courtesy. Invariably most of his talks concerned his combat experience, and as time went on, with memory growing a bit dim but nostalgia and enthusiasm just growing, he would tell about how he charged with Pickett at Gettysburg and then describe the surrender at Vicksburg, despite the fact that he could not possibly have attended both events on that same July day. However, nobody ever objected. After all, why let a few statistics spoil a good speech? Especially after forty years of telling it all so well. Fiction or non-fiction, the art was what counted. Both the old captain and his audience knew that.

Next on the program beside the new bridge was the baptizing. Butler's Hole was the name of a deep place in the creek, and the Hole was used for drinking water whenever drought struck the neighborhood. Today, however, the Hole was for baptism, and the eight-foot-high bank added to the

drama of the moment as Parson Terry raised his arms and
fists to heaven and shouted the full repertoire of all his Baptist convictions of fire and brimstone upon whoever did not
descend into the water with him.

Lustily leading the singing of "How Firm a Foundation,"
Brother Terry momentarily forgot himself, stepped back and
vanished from sight over the edge of the embankment.

After the splash, he rose to the surface and, nothing daunted,
motioned to his followers to join him as the spirit moved them.
It was one of the most successful baptizings in anybody's
recollection.

In fact, Uncle Charles Fowler was so moved by it all that
he even went over to the book peddler and offered to shake
hands and buy a copy of *Pilgrim's Progress*. Not to be outdone,
the badly battered salesman let him have the $7.50 morocco-
bound edition for $5.00. Everybody cheered this commendable
end of hostilities, and a traveling photographer in the crowd
who specialized in family "Groupees" took a picture of the
two men shaking hands and holding both the book and the
five-dollar bill.

The Fowlers always kept the book next to the family album
and Bible on the parlor table in front of the horsehair sofa.
One irreverent descendant contended that this was done not so
much as a reminder of the bridge-raising and Uncle Charles'
conversion as it was to preserve proof of at least one outstanding bargain among his investments.

* * *

As a matter of fact, certain aspects of religious practice
supplied more social activity than anything else in the Red
River Valley communities before the turn of the century.
In this connection, nothing seemed to generate more interest
than the religous debates.

One such debate began with a toothache, for if A. D.
Lennox had not had to go to the dental office of Dr. Nix in
Detroit, this story would never have happened.

to both Morrill and DeMorse as "Yankees," acknowledging rather grudgingly the editor as the lesser of two such evils in the community. He also firmly stated his refusal at one time to cooperate with Morrill in a suit to obtain the freedom of a Negro girl.

When at last all the evidence was heard, Judge Todd gave his fully detailed charge to the jury. In a remarkably short time they returned with their verdict which was in favor of Amos Morrill, but the amount was reduced from $20,000 to $8,000.

At once Morrill sprang to his feet, expressed his appreciation of their justice, and then with characteristic impulse of beau geste he remitted all the damages awarded, accepting only the payment for actual court costs.

It was over, and despite the prejudice against him, he had won and vindicated himself. It was no small triumph in his strife-torn career.

Later in the year he was charged in Lamar County with passing counterfeit money. He demanded a jury trial and again was acquitted. Still his enemies kept after him, and he was charged with perjury. Yet again he was tried and acquitted.

Morrill obviously recognized that it was time for him to move, and he did. He went to Austin and formed a law partnership with Andrew Jackson Hamilton, who was later to become governor of Texas and who shared Morrill's political thinking against secession.

In Austin the Morrills built a two-story stone mansion, above the north bank of the Colorado River, but their enjoyment of their new home was brief. The feeling about secession was making it unhealthy for any Unionist sympathizer. Civil war was upon the country.

Amos Morrill went to Mexico and then to Massachusetts. While he was in New England in 1864 his alma mater Bowdoin College conferred a Master of Arts degree upon him.

However, nothing could have been more indicative of Morrill's emotional ties than the fact that as soon as Union forces captured New Orleans he went there, and as soon as the war was over he returned to Austin. He had not believed in the Confederacy, but he believed in Texas.

When General Sheridan appointed E. M. Pease as Governor of Texas, Pease appointed Amos Morrill Chief Justice of the Supreme Court in 1868. Four years later President Grant appointed him Federal Judge of the Eastern District of Texas. As a jurist his record of decisions was memorable for the brilliance which had always attracted so much admiration and an equal measure of irritation. To him the law was thunder and lightning, and he rode the storm with a strange combination of dignity and delight.

There were persons who always wondered why an enemy did not kill him. It would seem that they feared his ghost would prosecute the case.

And so it was that in the seventy-fifth year of his life and in the setting he loved best, at home in Austin in view of the Capitol, Judge Morrill rested his case.

15.

Fun For Free

PERHAPS the most memorable entertainment of all was relished by the Red River folks when it accompanied events not usually listed in the entertainment field. One of the most popular of these amusements was "bridge-raising."

At first while the land was being settled, most of the many creeks were crossed by simply putting logs down in the creek beds and then trusting to luck that horses' feet and the wheels of wagon or carriage would not get caught, slip, and break. But in time as settlement steadily increased, of course a tax was levied for road and bridge building. Part of this money came from the county and most of it from the men who would benefit from such improvements in the area of their homes, farms, and businesses.

When a real bridge was built, the achievement of the finished product to aid transportation and travel was celebrated with a ceremony and party. A good example was the affair which the Bowers family of three generations ago planned when a bridge was built across Langford Creek, some five miles south of Clarksville.

This was to be a bridge-raising that would go down in the social records of 1893 as just about the ultimate, for the gentlemen who were the hosts arranged to combine a fish fry, a public speaking, and a baptizing for their guests.

Several miles south of the new bridge was Turner's Lake, and they seined that in order to get hundreds of pounds of fresh catfish. When the guests arrived they could smell the fish cooking in four huge iron vats filled with boiling grease out in the pasture. Vast slabs of cornbread were cooking, a steer was barbecued, and seemingly endless kettles of coffee were boiling between the long tables set up to accommodate the crowd.

One of the most popular men in the region arrived with his usual flourish of personality. He was Uncle Charles Fowler. Neatly, almost nattily groomed from his boots to his little black goatee, he cut quite a figure as he called greetings right and left. In fact, folks often wondered why and how Uncle Charles kept out of politics. With a high temper always geared and ready for a fight or frolic, he was never in the background where any audience assembled.

Today was no exception as he spied a stranger in the crowd, strode over to him, and let go a good right to the man's jaw.

Everybody was delighted with the prospect of so much excitement to spark the party. Here was a good fight to enjoy and explanations could come later.

Meanwhile the stranger, who was said to be a book sales-man, recovered himself and returned the attack. He went into a clinch with Uncle Charles and managed to get a firm grip on the Fowler goatee. Down they both went in what was called a "tom cat roll" which finally became so violent that they had to be pulled apart. By then half of Uncle Charles' goatee was gone, and the stranger had a good part of his ear bitten off. Everyone agreed that it was as fine a "wool pulling" and "onion skinning" as any professionals could have exhibited.

While the principals were given first aid, Uncle Charles explained that the peddler had been at his house the day before and forced his way in, trying to sell a copy of *Pilgrim's Progress*. This had annoyed Aunt Becky Fowler, and when Uncle Charles came in from the garden to rescue her from this hard-sell disciple of John Bunyan, he had to make a "razoo" at the fellow with a grubbing hoe to get rid of him.

Naturally, the sight of the offender here among a social gathering was a signal for action.

Now that the fight was over, they all had a fine appetite, and dinner was served in heaping platters and mugs. Brother Terry, the Baptist parson, was called upon to return thanks. He took out his Waterbury watch and prayed for ten minutes. After that it was every man, woman, and child for himself. Everybody ate too much, thoroughly relished it, and considered a spoon of soda afterwards a small price to pay for such a magnificent heartburn.

After dinner the program featured Captain Thomas, a lawyer with quite a reputation for oratory. As his admirers said, "He could really put the dew on the violets."

An ex-Confederate officer of course, Capt. Thomas was something of a rarity, because his military title was entirely bona fide and not a matter of courtesy. Invariably most of his talks concerned his combat experience, and as time went on, with memory growing a bit dim but nostalgia and enthusiasm just growing, he would tell about how he charged with Pickett at Gettysburg and then describe the surrender at Vicksburg, despite the fact that he could not possibly have attended both events on that same July day. However, nobody ever objected. After all, why let a few statistics spoil a good speech? Especially after forty years of telling it all so well. Fiction or non-fiction, the art was what counted. Both the old captain and his audience knew that.

Next on the program beside the new bridge was the baptizing. Butler's Hole was the name of a deep place in the creek, and the Hole was used for drinking water whenever drought struck the neighborhood. Today, however, the Hole was for baptism, and the eight-foot-high bank added to the drama of the moment as Parson Terry raised his arms and fists to heaven and shouted the full repertoire of all his Baptist convictions of fire and brimstone upon whoever did not descend into the water with him.

Lustily leading the singing of "How Firm a Foundation," Brother Terry momentarily forgot himself, stepped back and vanished from sight over the edge of the embankment.

After the splash, he rose to the surface and, nothing daunted, motioned to his followers to join him as the spirit moved them. It was one of the most successful baptizings in anybody's recollection.

In fact, Uncle Charles Fowler was so moved by it all that he even went over to the book peddler and offered to shake hands and buy a copy of *Pilgrim's Progress.* Not to be outdone, the badly battered salesman let him have the $7.50 morocco-bound edition for $5.00. Everybody cheered this commendable end of hostilities, and a traveling photographer in the crowd who specialized in family "Groupees" took a picture of the two men shaking hands and holding both the book and the five-dollar bill.

The Fowlers always kept the book next to the family album and Bible on the parlor table in front of the horsehair sofa. One irreverent descendant contended that this was done not so much as a reminder of the bridge-raising and Uncle Charles' conversion as it was to preserve proof of at least one outstanding bargain among his investments.

* * *

As a matter of fact, certain aspects of religious practice supplied more social activity than anything else in the Red River Valley communities before the turn of the century. In this connection, nothing seemed to generate more interest than the religous debates.

One such debate began with a toothache, for if A. D. Lennox had not had to go to the dental office of Dr. Nix in Detroit, this story would never have happened.

The dentist chatted away with his patient, and to get his mind off the sore tooth he hold Lennox that the Campbellites were planning a big meeting at what was called the Grove Tabernacle just south of town. This meeting would feature a preacher named Absalom Andrews, and Brother Andrews had issued a challenge for anybody to meet him in debate. But he preferred a Baptist because be believed that the Baptists were in more error than any other church.

As a Baptist, Dr. Nix felt that a challenger should be provided who would mow this man down in proper fashion. What's more, the dentist knew a preacher equal to this emergency. He was Brother Pennington, who lived in Fannin County and was famed as a rip-snorting debater with an especially violent aversion to Campbellites.

To bring these two men together with the full artillery of all their principles, prejudices, and showmanship would be the event of the year. Lennox agreed as best he could with his mouth open, and as soon as he was out of the chair he wrote the letter of invitation to Parson Pennington as the dentist suggested.

In another week or so Lennox was in town again, this time at the pool hall. But before he could begin to enjoy a game, someone came in to tell him that an elderly man with a white beard and a West Tennessee grip had arrived in town and was looking for Brother Lennox.

At once he slipped out the back door, jumped in the saddle, and rode home. Later at supper he heard a buggy drive up, and, of course, there were Dr. Nix and Brother Pennington. He joined them, and off they went to the Grove Tabernacle.

Inside they sat down on the side with the men, for with utmost orthodoxy the seating separated the sexes.

Parson Andrews was well into his sermon, and as usual at the climax he hurled his challenge for anyone to debate. Now Parson Pennington rose, buttoned the flap of his stiff bosom shirt even more securely, and shouted his acceptance.

Each man glared at the other and took eager measurement

for a moment while the congregation whispered and nudged each other in delight.

The meeting was quickly concluded, and then the conference was held to set the next evening at 7:30 P.M. for opening the debate. Rules also had to be decided upon, with a couple of Brother Andrews' deacons and Brother Pennington's colleagues Dr. Nix and Lennox serving as seconds to arrange the verbal duel.

Most important was official protection to insure a fair division of the offering plate collections, so that the champions could cover their expenses perhaps with profit as well as glory.

It was soon established that they agreed upon nothing at all except the mode of baptism (immersion in water) and the King James translation of the Bible.

Personally they shared a lifelong fondness for fried chicken and a great dislike for both the Catholic and Episcopal clergy. They distrusted the priests because they could not understand their Latin, and they hated the Episcopal rectors because they could understand them and this was even worse.

Reports flew like chicken feathers about the headstrong views of these mighty warriors of the gospel who were out to slay each other, and people filled the tabernacle to overflowing. Many stood outside in the grove with the children and dogs.

The meeting began on time as each preacher was introduced and rose to bow and be seen by everybody inside and at the doors and windows.

Brother Pennington was very tall, and his white beard gave him added dignity. His voice could almost be heard across the Big Red and into the Territory, for he was the proud possessor of several hog-calling contest medals. Here was a veteran.

But Brother Andrews was sparked by the confidence of youth and through his soupstrainer mustache came a shrill and piercing volume of sound which might not shake the rafters but could rattle the window panes.

Both men had command of an Anglo-Saxon vocabulary perfectly suited to the hostilities involved. Each knew the Bible practically by heart, and there was sheer fascination in hearing them repeat the same words and interpret them so differently that it was impossible to tell black from white and be really sure about it. Of course, this amused the Methodists and members of other churches in the audience because to them it just showed how confused and wrong both the Baptists and the Campbellites were. As result, everybody was happily reinforced in his own sectarian way and positive that his facet of Truth was right.

Night after night on text after text the debate went on and attracted more and more people who drove and rode in from miles around. Finally it had to be moved out of the tabernacle and into the old Harrow factory building in town. Partisan feeling ran fever high, and there were an impressive number of fist fights as side attractions.

Finally a couple of Campbellites decided that something had to conclude the endless debate and that only strategy could do it. Accordingly, they went to an old lady, a Baptist, and after considerable conversation and bestowal of a very substantial sum of money which would remove any financial worry for her for the future, a deal was made.

The following evening about halfway through the debate, this little white-haired lady rose and declared in no uncertain terms that she was a lifelong Baptist and had been here every night but now was convinced by Brother Absalom Andrews that it was time to change to the right church. She would withdraw her letter and become a Campbellite.

This was a dramatic moment, and in the excitement Brother Pennington pocketed his part of the collection and some cold fried chicken and left town, never to return.

The debate was over, but not the ill feelings and hatred it had generated.

Years later the men who had negotiated the old lady's "conversion" confessed the story. But by then it was too late.

She was gone. The damage was done, and nobody seemed to care. The "joke" had misfired.

* * *

Still other uses and abuses of religion are among the old records in the Red River courthouse, and one story was sensational enough to supply a decade's conversation.

It began in 1884 when a young lawyer, H. B. Wright, came to Clarksville and put out his shingle. He did well, especially as local agent for the Texas Land and Loan Company of Galveston. Capital was scarce along the Red River, and planters and businessmen welcomed the chance to borrow money at ten percent interest, which was considered a reasonable rate. Spurred by this success, Wright opened an abstract office to clear titles.

After several years, however, the Galveston company noticed a few errors, discrepancies and inconsistencies in his rather complicated reports. They became suspicious and secretly engaged another lawyer in Clarksville, Mr. Henry Lennox, to investigate Mr. Wright's activities which were growing larger and larger in scale. Accordingly, Mr. Lennox's research required the utmost discretion and ingenuity, for the most difficult assignment in any small town is to maintain a secret. Both men were laboring under this same handicap, but from opposite directions and purposes.

Gradually Wright sensed that somebody was checking on him. The fact that he was engaged in fraudulent operations involving some very clever forgeries tended to keep him especially alert. But it would take a man just as clever to find these things out, and Mr. Wright, of course, doubted that any such man existed.

But as the days went by, his ego began to weaken and he began to suspect that Mr. Lennox was on his trail. For proof Wright devised a scheme which could hardly fail.

The Baptists were holding a big revival meeting, and Wright knew that Lennox was a very devout deacon in the church.

Never having joined this church nor any other, Wright saw the chance now to have religion serve him most effectively.

The night of May 15, 1891, was a very stormy one with a high wind blowing, but despite the weather Wright went to the Baptist revival, and when the preacher called for converts, Wright was the first one on his feet to walk down the aisle toward the altar and salvation. At once the deacons came forward to extend "the right hand of fellowship," which all of them did as usual—except Mr. Lennox.

This gave the "convert" the proof he needed, and as if to help the sinner more, the wind blew out the kerosene lamps in the church. When they were lighted again, behold— Brother Wright was not there.

He disappeared not only from the church but from the town and the entire area and was never seen nor heard of again.

When the fall term of District Court convened, a grand jury brought in thirteen indictments against him for forgery and embezzlement. Warrants were issued for his arrest, but none could ever be served on him.

The old diary of W. M. Bowers records the incident simply and succinctly: "Our little lawyer Wright caught up with at last. He got into the people to the amount of $40,000.00 and run off and left the people the bag to hold until he drives the snipes in but God knows when he will be back with the snipes."

16.

Politics, Texas Style

POLITICS have always been thought to have a notably flamboyant quality in the area where America's old South and new West came together in Texas, and never was this more true than in the 1880's and 1890's, especially in the Red River country.

Men took their politics seriously, and women enjoyed the entertainment value, and the politicians enjoyed themselves. Ability was a matter of oratory, showmanship, and violent hostility. For the citizen-spectator it was a sport which drew the partisan support and enthusiasm to be expressed in later years at the baseball park and football stadium.

The year 1880 saw an election of such vehemence in Red River County that the reports were handed down to the generations who followed. It was only a routine race for the state legislature, but despite the poor pay involved, the office had somehow attracted the interest of two very prominent men to compete for it. One was Captain Jim Clark, son of the man for whom Clarksville was named, and the other was Mack Bailey of Detroit in the western part of the county.

Though the election was not until September, the campaign began in May. By July the fury of the contest was equal to the midsummer temperature.

As one diary records:

July 19, 1888—Sylvester Harmon and Gus Shaw clawed each other's manes about Clark and Bailey.

July 30, 1888—Charley Miers and Felin Fox had a wool-pulling about Clark and Bailey. Fox got up twice but stayed down the third time.

September 17, 1888—The Campaign wound up with the most devilish riot I ever witnessed in all my life.

September 21, 1888—Election came off. Bailey beat Clark 77 votes.

*   *   *

Four years later Clarksville was the scene of an event which was remembered for another reason, as Governor James Stephen Hogg came to deliver a speech of special importance to people suffering the economic ills of cheap cotton.

Big preparations were made to welcome the governor. A brass band was imported, and the Red River Rifles, a crack company of local military which included the young lawyer John Nance Garner, marched to the railroad station to meet Governor Hogg and escort him around the square.

The Governor and his reception committee had seats of honor in a victoria carriage drawn by two horses. The procession ended at the courthouse where he was to speak from the judge's bench in the courtroom.

Just as he rose to begin, a lady by the name of Mrs. Belle Morrison went up and presented him with a large drinking gourd.

He spoke eloquently in thanking her, saying that just such a gourd was what he had always wanted and that if it were solid gold he could not prize it more. Then as a climax he declared, "I would rather have a drink of water out of this gourd than a three column puff in the *Dallas News.*"

After his official speech the governor was escorted back to the station with the band and honor guard. With his hat in one hand and the gourd in the other, he waved farewell as the train pulled out to the east.

But a few minutes later when the train was safely beyond the town, he went to a window and threw the gourd out as far as his enormous strength could hurl it, returning to his seat with a sigh of relief to be rid of it.

Most unfortunately, however, as political bad luck would have it, the field in which the gourd landed was Mrs. Morrison's pasture, and one of her Negro workers picked it up and brought it to her when she got home.

The story went through the county, and it was generally agreed that heads of state should use more discretion in disposal of gifts if they were interested in support at the polls.

Naturally, Governor Hogg's name was one which could easily be used and abused by wits and punsters into all manner of uncomplimentary references to its barnyard counterpart, and the popular pastime of misspelling it gained favor among Mrs. Morrison's social circle.

* * *

The characteristic of a more or less rugged individualism always seemed to flow along the Red River, and a rather striking instance of this was evident when the first election was held to vote on establishing a free public school system in Clarksville.

This was in 1889, and the idea met with much resistance. After all, there were private schools where the families with children paid for their instruction, and these parents were outraged by the thought of a tax to offer free education to other people's children.

When the votes were counted, the result was that the school tax was defeated.

Governor Hogg visited Clarksville on May 7, 1892. The local military company which escorted him from the station and around the square included law student John Nance Garner. The commander, Morgan Graves, is standing in front of the flag. Gov. Hogg is seated in the open victoria with Col. Sam E. Watson on his left. In front of Gov. Hogg is Col. Shaw. George McCulloch is driving the victoria and Ferdinand Greiner is on his left. The courthouse is in the far background of the picture. Note how muddy the square is.

An excerpt from the Bowers diary states the majority opinion.

April 2, 1889—We beat the unjust school tax that our little bob-tail corporation tried so hard to vote us on. It was to school their brats that we had no hand in begetting. He that dances must pay the fiddler is my doctrine.

17.

The Sporting Life

A N old-timer of the region offers as his opinion that one reason for the Red River's color is that it is blushing for the goings-on which took place along its southern shore back in the days when America was moving its frontier to the southwest.

Certainly the records show that early in the Republic of Texas, at least in Red River settlements, the gambling instinct expressed itself in every way that the law did and did not allow.

Horse racing was one of the most popular sports in that pioneer society. In fact, one of the first race tracks in Texas was laid out near Jonesboro in 1837, and there are still traces of that track to be seen. Later tracks were also built at Clarksville and at Boston in Bowie County.

A doctor of Clarksville, W. F. T. Hart, became a leading sportsman in Texas with his famous stallion named Albert Gallatin, a name chosen to commemorate the doctor's admiration of Thomas Jefferson's Secretary of the Treasury.

Dr. Hart had need of an astute treasurer himself, for his passion for racing kept his own finances in considerable peril most of the time. As result, he was in more or less constant litigation with some sixty-eight lawsuits from 1841 to 1873, and his horse spent as much time in the sheriff's stable as it did at home.

Gambling on horse racing was well advertised. For example, there was this ad in the *Clarksville Northern Standard* of November 6, 1844:

Hart and Co. are hereby notified that my horse Woodpecker can take their horse Albert Gallatin, two mile heats over the Boston track on the 1st Monday next May for a negro boy worth $650.00 and also $350.00 cash. The objection I have to the Clarksville track is that it is too muddy in wet weather and too hard in dry weather.

Signed: C. E. Hilburn

Without any laws or racing commissions to regulate the sport as a gambling medium, naturally there was a good deal of crooked practice. Much of this came to court in the form of lawsuits on claims of fraud, such as misrepresenting the age of horses and whether the horses were tried or untried in racing. Many of these cases were settled out of court, and a number of defendants simply got on their fast horses and rode out of Texas.

By 1840 the gambling fever was at a peak, and the favorite way of winning and losing money was neither on horses nor on poker. It was Faro. At that time the game was played with a very simple layout and not at all like the elaborate setup which later developed.

Losses became so fantastic that finally the most stringent laws were passed in order to get the situation under control.

When the grand jury of Red River County met in 1840, over thirty indictments were brought in against "gambling at Faro," "keeping a Faro table," "betting on a Faro bank," etc. Many of the indictments were against some of the most prominent men south of the Red River.

In reaction and in an attempt to by-pass the laws, a new

game was introduced called Forty-Eight, but it was only a variation of Faro, played with forty-eight cards instead of fifty-two. They simply removed the four sevens from the deck. A case of some special interest came up as Number 58, October 9, 1840, *The Republic of Texas vs. Asa Jarman.* Mr. Jarman was indicted for keeping a gaming table for playing Forty-Eight, the banking game equivalent to Faro. He was found guilty. He appealed the case, but while the appeal was pending, another indictment was brought against him, this time for adultery. His partner in that offense was one Elizabeth Martin.

Asa Jarman decided that all added up to a little too much legal confusion at one time. He settled both matters very simply. He and Elizabeth packed up and left the Republic of Texas. The frontier was becoming too regulated for a man of his multiple activities and interests.

As a matter of fact, adultery was a very commonplace offense enjoyed not only by the participants but also the peace officers of the time, because on the fee system which operated then, they could collect on two culprits instead of just one.

The records of District Court of Red River County show more charges of the crime of the Scarlet Letter filed in the spring term of 1840 than for the entire thirty years from 1927 to 1957. Whatever conclusions can be drawn from this fact are at the readers' risk, not the authors'.

18.

Anchors Aweigh

From the 1820's until the early 1870's the settlers along the Red River were as dependent on the steamboats as were the planters beside the Mississippi. The only difference was that traffic and travel on the Big Red had its seasonal uncertainties. At times the river was kept churning with traffic. When the dry spells came, the boats and their crew and cargo and passengers had to wait, and while they waited in port quite a few things happened, including lawsuits.

Sometimes, however, not shallow water but overflow caused trouble on this temperamental waterway. The results are buried treasures which still offer a haunting challenge to those who have heard the stories.

No such story has held more frustrating fascination for well over a century now than the one about the steamboat which was sunk with a cargo of 300 barrels of whiskey.

Duly insured and with whiskey at only sixty-five cents a gallon then, the owners and underwriters did not face too great a loss. But as the years went by and men began thinking about how mellow and "ropey" that whiskey was becoming as it aged in those stout oak barrels in the sand somewhere under the river, plus the increase in its value, they began diving down among the catfish to try to find the lost ship and that attractive cargo.

Nobody has ever found it. The channel has changed and nobody even knows where to look for it. But the possibility remains a phantom pleasure to contemplate when the Red takes on an amber look.

Jonesboro, Rowland, Mrs. Gaffney's Landing, and Pecan Point were the major Texas ports, and it was at Mrs. Gaffney's Landing that Captain James Broadwell as master and owner of the steamboat *LaFitte* got into difficulties.

He had docked there on May 1, 1859, to load 500 bales of cotton bound for New Orleans. With that weight cargo the *LaFitte* had a draft of three and a half feet, and higher water was needed to float her off down the river.

For a week Captain Broadwell had waited for the river to rise, when John Pasley visited him and demanded payment of a note for $1400. This note the captain had given for Mr. Pasley's half-interest in the *LaFitte*. Broadwell knew that the note was due, but it had been made out to be payable in New Orleans. As soon as this cargo reached New Orleans and sold at $5.00 freight a bale, the note would be paid. It was just a matter of waiting for the river to rise.

Mr. Pasley refused to cooperate with the vagaries of the river. He announced that he was riding to Clarksville to engage a lawyer to bring suit and tie up the boat by writ of attachment.

Captain Broadwell paced the deck, swore, and watched the river. Early in the morning of May 10th he noted the rise and ordered his engineer to get up steam. At eleven o'clock the boat was ready to cast off, but just as the gangplank was to be lifted, a man ran aboard. He was a deputy sheriff of Red River County and he had the writ of attachment. If his horse had even so much as stumbled a time or two on the ride from Clarksville, the *LaFitte* would have been on its way.

Now it stayed in port while Captain Broadwell went ashore

and arranged to post a cash bond of $1500. By the time he had managed to get and put up the money, the river had fallen again. No more disgusted man ever paced a deck beside any shore.

Finally on May 24th the river rose again and with full steam up he was able to steer the *LaFitte* away from Mrs. Gaffney's Landing. But he did not get very far away, for at the mouth of Black Bayou the boat was grounded, stranded, wrecked.

Captain Broadwell and his crew rowed to the Texas shore and went to Clarksville to defend his case and cause. There they were joined by other men from other ships, the *Osceola,* the *Hope,* the *Era,* the *Trio,* the *Ham Howell,* all of them suffering the same fate on the tricky Big Red. All of them testified that the upper river was navigable but "always dangerous," even for experienced pilots and even when boats were passed and certified by the Inspectors of the Board of Underwriters in New Orleans. They angrily denied that "old boats are sent there to be sunk."

Captain Broadwell's case dragged on for seven years. Finally it was dismissed with a notation which must have been written by a satirist lost to American literature, for the notation ready, "Dismissed at the suggestion of the defendant."

By 1866 the Texas court had decided that, after all, this case came under the jurisdiction of New Orleans. Such conclusions took time. Why hurry? The river didn't.

* * *

The Billy Clark family of Red River County has preserved the old shipping book from the years 1860, 1861, and 1866 which Rowland T. Bryarly used at the port of Old Rowland, which he had founded in 1838.

A separate entry was recorded for every shipment of cotton out of the port. The cost of loading the bales from the landing on the ships was approximately thirty-three cents a bale if a good quantity was to be handled. If only one or a few bales were to be loaded on the river boats, the price increased to more than a dollar a bale.

The following is a summary of the shipping book information:

DATE	TYPE CRAFT	NAME	BALES	DESTINATION
Jan. 19, 1860	Steam ship	Trio	496	New Orleans
Feb. 5, 1860	Steam ship	News Boy	138	New Orleans
Feb. 6, 1860	Steamer	Martin Walt	44	New Orleans
Feb. 8, 1860	Steam boat	Era #3	635	New Orleans
Feb. 11, 1860	Steamer	Arkansaw	333	New Orleans
Feb. 19, 1860	Steamer	Era #2	243	New Orleans
Feb. 22, 1860	Steamer	Riseu	74	New Orleans
Feb. 23, 1860	Steam boat	Martin Walt	162	New Orleans
Mar. 3, 1860	Steamer	Era #4	188	New Orleans
Mar. 6, 1860	Steamer	Rescue	51	New Orleans
Mar. 20, 1860	Steamer	Rescue	115*	Shreveport

*This entry also records that several "chests" were shipped to Shreveport with the bales of cotton. This is the only time anything but cotton was listed in the book.

Feb. 7, 1861	Steamer	W. S. Johnson	317	New Orleans
Mar. 18, 1861	Steamer	Era #6	104	New Orleans
Apr. 1, 1861	flat boat	Bill Yancy	78	New Orleans
Apr. 10, 1861	Steamer	Fannie Pearson	33	New Orleans
Apr. 10, 1861	Steamer	Wm. M. Levy	887	New Orleans
Apr. 12, 1861	Steamer	Vigo	137	New Orleans
Mar. 24, 1866	flat boat	Ruley White	107	Shreveport
Mar. 25, 1866	Steam boat	George	338	Shreveport
May 6, 1866	Steam boat	George	49	New Orleans
May 15, 1866	Steam boat	The Texas	7	New Orleans
May 16, 1866	(illegible)	(illegible)	10	New Orleans
May 25, 1866	Steam boat	George	23	New Orleans

Compiled by John D. Osburn, Clarksville.

19.

The Iron Horse Comes

BEFORE 1832 a trail road had been blazed from the river port of Jonesboro southward to the old town of Nacogdoches which was on the Spanish Trail, and when Sam Houston first entered Texas and traveled that road out of Jonesboro, the report was that he saw only two houses along the entire distance. That was well over 200 miles.

A major problem for any development of settlements was going to be transportation. The river, as we have seen, was all too often unreliable. At first, of course, when hunting and trapping for furs and hides was the only commerce, the problem was slight. Later, however, when planters came, it was a long waiting period for them indeed to get the proceeds from the sale of their cotton in New Orleans, after transporting it by ox wagon to the river ports of Jonesboro or Jefferson.

Accordingly, the dream of a railroad coming into Texas was the constant hope of the planter and merchant on this frontier. On February 7, 1853, when the Memphis, El Paso, and Pacific Railroad Company (a name of grandiose conception) was incorporated by the Texas legislature, the dream began taking exciting shape. But the Civil War years halted that construction.

On June 12, 1873, the doomed Memphis, El Paso, and Pacific Company was sold under foreclosure to the Texas and Pacific Railway for $150,000, and later on construction got under way again. The survey called for this railroad to begin at Nash, just west of Texarkana, and pass through Clarksville, Paris, Bonham, Sherman, and then turn south to Ft. Worth.

Building gangs began working from Nash westward and from Sherman eastward, and on August 10, 1876, the rails were joined together at exactly 5:40 P.M. at a point twenty-three miles east of Clarksville.

Celebrations of this event were held up and down the lines, especially at Clarksville, where the first train was expected to come through on its trial run sometime Saturday afternoon, August 12th.

No actual schedule was possible because the railroad men themselves could not figure how fast the engine would run on several of the difficult grades on the line.

However, time was not of the essence in Clarksville, and festivity was. Nobody cared when the train arrived as long as it got there. The saloons were filled, especially with the construction workmen. People gathered all along the new track after very carefully taking their horses out of wagon and hack harness and hitching them at a safe distance.

But the horses were not the only creatures never to have seen a railroad train before. For most of the men, women, and children it was a new experience too.

At last about 4:30 P.M. they saw smoke in the distance and finally the whistle was heard. Everybody screamed and yelled and waved flags, signs of welcome and congratulations, handkerchiefs, and whatever was available.

The train rolled in and came to a stop, cinders flying. High officials of the railroad descended, listened to the mayor's speech, and responded with their own speeches which had just been given at DeKalb and would be delivered again at Paris, Bonham, and Sherman with increasing gusto.

Then people were invited to come on the train and inspect its interior. After this, the conductor shouted his proud "All Aboard," the engineer and fireman rang the bell and blew the whistle, and with much puffiing and chugging the train pulled out in trailing clouds of smoke and glory.

People began telling each other goodbye and relaxing from all the excitement, drifting off toward their horses to hitch them up again for the rides home. Then suddenly smoke was seen reappearing on the western horizon, and to their amazement they saw the train returning!

So much steam had been used by the engineer in the ceremonial whistle-tooting that when the train came to Campbell's Grade a couple of miles west, the engine could not pull the grade and so had to back up to the Clarksville station, gather its strength, and start off again. This time they made it, but for quite a while the people waited to see what would happen and to make a few bets on the side.

Above: *This Texas and Pacific locomotive is similar to the little steam engine which made the first run through Clarksville in 1876.* Below: *Page's Tree stands peacefully today in the Clarksville cemetery. But 120 years or more ago it was The Hanging Tree, and served the cause of "justice" as the local execution spot. (See chapter 21.)*

20.

Robert Potter and
"The Lion of the Lakes"

WHEN court was formally called to order in the log court-house on the Clarksville square on the morning of March 23, 1840, the room was jammed to an unusual degree of overflowing with officials, lawyers, and spectators eager to see and hear a new member of the bar who was a national celebrity in more ways than one.

He was not only famous, he was infamous. He was Robert Potter of North Carolina and Texas.

Women wanted to get a glimpse of his charm and no-toriously dark good looks. Men were just as anxious to observe the manner and oratory of a man who had talked his way out of prison for an act which had added a new word to the language of crime. Besides, Col. Potter had already crowded into his forty years of violent vigor the historic honor of being a signer of the Declaration of Independence of the Republic of Texas and having served as Secretary of the Texas Navy.

If he was aware of the sensation he was causing, his social expertise gave no indication of it. After all, he was used to such attention from both men and women. Dressed in flawlessly good taste, he sat chatting with two men he had just met, John Denton and Capt. William Rose, none of them knowing how soon this introductory friendship would turn into hatred.

Back of them, people went on whispering, for even in that day of delayed communications, everyone knew what had changed the scene of Robert Potter's brilliant career in politics.

In the Wheeler *History of North Carolina* there was this grandiose bit of restraint in recording him:

Robert Potter was a resident and representative from Granville County. I once thought after I had prepared a sketch of him that I would omit it and pass in silence the name of one who had been a member of this county in the Assembly and the Representative of his district in Congress. But truth demands that not only the good should be noted but those who have been notorious for other qualities. This, too, may have a moral effect.

Robert Potter was a man of no ordinary powers of intellect. With an address which would have graced the most polished court in Europe, with powers of eloquence that could command all listening auditors and sway them to his will, and an energy that shrunk from no obstacles or opposition, had his fierce and ferocious temper been tamed by parental persuasion, his name might have stood "high on the dusty rolls which ages keep."

What was all the mystery? The story was too big for secrecy.

Robert Potter was born in June, 1799, in Granville County, North Carolina. When he was only fifteen he was appointed midshipman in the U.S. Navy and served for six years. After that he went to Halifax in his home state and studied law in the office of Thomas Burgess, an attorney of prominence there. Potter was handsome, gifted, and ambitious, gallant with the ladies and not afraid of the devil himself among men. It was inevitable that he should get into politics. He was a natural magnet for it.

On the local scene in Halifax there were two political factions—one led by young Potter's friend Burgess, and the other by a man named Thomas Bynum. A feud developed between

Bynum and Potter when Mr. Bynum made the mistake of socially snubbing him. At once Potter challenged Bynum to a duel which Bynum refused. Duels were between gentlemen, and Bynum said that this qualification eliminated his challenger. Potter's reply was to post placards all over town to the effect that Bynum was "a poltroon and coward." The stage was set for an election campaign of more than usual interest.

In 1825 they both announced as candidates for the North Carolina House of Commons. The campaign came to a climax in a free-for-all fight in which Potter was stabbed with a sword cane, Bynum's head was broken with a club, and another man was killed. The election was called off and declared void, and Halifax remained unrepresented in the legislature that year while everyone recovered.

In 1826 Robert Potter ran again against the Bynum party. This time he won the election, though the opponents went on claiming fraud. Two years later he was reelected.

In the House he further made himself a figure of controversy as he introduced measures for education which were far in advance of the time.

The next election in 1827 he lost, and he left Halifax to return to Granville. Behind him, however, he left a poem in circulation which he had entitled, "The Head of Medusa, a Mock Heroic Poem by Rienzi." In it was all the literary evidence of his low opinion of the city fathers. The Greeks had nothing on Robert Potter when his ire was burning.

In the summer of 1828 he was elected to the United States House of Representatives. As congressman he served with impressive distinction for three years and appeared to be destined next for the Senate. But in the summer of 1831 he committed the crime which ever since has been known as "Potterizing."

He was married to Isabella Taylor, the daughter of a prominent family, and they had two children. Mrs. Potter was very active in Methodist Church work, and he became jealous and suspicious of her close association with the minister, Rev.

Louis Taylor, a second cousin of hers. Potter also became suspicious of her close friendship with another relative, Louis Wiley. Taylor was about fifty, and Wiley was seventeen. The range in age was rather comprehensive for adultery.

On evidence which was sufficient for Potter, he accused Taylor, beat him, and castrated him. Then he went to Wiley's home and likewise emasculated him.

Potter was tried and sentenced to two years' imprisonment and a thousand-dollar fine. His defense, of course, had been the "Unwritten Law," and no doubt if he had shot the men concerned, the verdict would have been more favorable. But the primitive originality of his revenge was a shock without precedent.

Even so, when he wrote an eighty-six page booklet in prison and had it printed, his "Address to the People of Granville County" (1832), in which he explained his defense even more fully, many men began to wonder if he had not indeed received an unjust sentence.

In addition, Potter used his prison window as a speaker's platform for continuing his political campaign, and people stood on the street outside to listen as his voice came dramatically through the bars. This was quite a fellow, they agreed; he had guts.

In the summer of 1834 they elected him to the House of Commons. Robert Potter was on his way again.

However, on Christmas night that year the nature of this man's complex vulnerability to passion caused another detour on that road to achievement. In the book *Nonnulla* by Joseph Blout Chesshire, published by the University of North Carolina Press, the story is told that Potter got into a card game that night with a member of the House from Cheatham County. The game was called "Thirteen the Odd," and the stakes were high. They played all night, and Potter lost all his money and all he could go out and borrow. By morning both men were exhausted. Potter pulled out a pistol, grabbed the money, and "thus got off with his booty."

After this episode he was expelled from the House of Commons by not too overwhelming a vote, 62 for expulsion and 42 against it. Obviously he still had many friends, but even so, a change of venue in his personal life seemed to be indicated. His friends suggested the current advice—"Go to Texas." The rough and tumble of frontier causes and opportunities could be an ideal environment for the Robert Potter temperament.

He arrived in Nacogdoches July 1, 1835, and a week later received his "certificate of character" there. He joined Capt. Thomas J. Rusk's Independent Volunteers and then was commissioned in the Texas Navy. His new life was begun with plenty of action. Texas was fighting, and Potter was a fighter. His friends had been right. He was in his element in this new country and its struggle.

In the winter of 1836 he was chosen to represent Nacogdoches as a delegate to the General Convention at Washington-on-the-Brazos where the Texas Declaration of Independence was written. With his signature fresh on that historic document he was elected Secretary of the Navy. A month later he was appointed Commander of the Port of Galveston. The tempo of events was fast and furious. Potter had opposed Sam Houston on every point of decision, especially concerning the Alamo. From now on the two men would make good enemies.

Robert Potter rode to Velasco to direct the frantic flight of refugee settlers and their families in what was known as the Runaway Scrape, so that at least the women and children would escape the onrush of the Mexican army and get to temporary safety on Galveston Island. But there on the coastal prairie he saw a woman with two little children, and the woman had the look of a lady who should not be in any such situation or condition at all. She was young and beautiful, and her fine skirt was spattered with mud from running over the miserable road. The children's faces were stained with the tears of fright and fatigue.

Col. Potter reined in his horse and dismounted and introduced himself. He had met the next great chapter in his fate, Harriet Moore Page, daughter of the well-known Dr. Francis Moore of Brazoria. No longer would she lack the proper escort and protection.

Harriet Ann was twenty-six years old at this time, and she too had had more than her share of experience crowded into those years.

Back home in Nashville before her father and stepmother had moved to Texas in answer to the call for physicians from his old friend Dr. Anson Jones, Harriet at seventeen had met Solomon Page. He seemed all that a suitor could be and after what for those days was a whirlwind courtship, they were married.

Her disillusionment was swift and complete. Her handsome husband was not the businessman he had represented himself to be to her family. He was a professional gambler, and their life drifted on the shifting sands of his luck and desperation. Missing the stability and respectability she had always known, and after the birth of a son and daughter, Harriet grimly took matters into her own hands. They had moved to New Orleans, and she went to work as a shopkeeper. The move to Texas was inevitable, as Solomon's next gamble. For Harriet it meant at least the relief of a reunion with her family and some unburdening of her loneliness and now hopeless problem.

The war in Texas gave Solomon Page a reason to desert his wife and children and do it as a hero instead of a scoundrel. He went off in the army, and that was the last heard of him until the war was over. Harriet found herself alone in a wilderness cabin with her children, an ordeal memorably described in her diary and related in even more detail in the outstanding biographical novel, *Love Is a Wild Assault.*[1]

This was the young woman in flight with her boy and baby girl, who seemed to have her faith restored when Col. Robert Potter rode up and rescued them.

---

[1]Elithe Hamilton Kirkland, *Love Is a Wild Assault* (New York: Doubleday and Company, 1959).

In Velasco, after getting Mrs. Page and her children aboard the schooner *Flash* and all other refugees ready for evacuation, Potter made frenzied efforts to fortify the port while messengers rode in with reports of more Mexican victories and the defeat and massacre of Texans. His new and very limited navy must fight off any supplies by sea to the Mexican army.

They sailed to Galveston to join forces with a half-dozen other ships, plus the American brig *Pocket,* which had been captured en route from New Orleans with cargo, equipment, and Mexican sailors commissioned by an agent of Santa Anna's.

Potter had Harriet Page and the children removed to the greater comfort of the prize ship *Pocket,* and it was there that her little daughter died. This sorrow embittered her more than ever toward the husband who had cared nothing for their welfare, and naturally the sympathy of Robert Potter meant more than ever to her.

Even the strain and stress of managing the rescue of President Burnet and other government officials of the new Republic of Texas so that temporary headquarters could be set up on Galveston Island could not keep Potter from devoting every possible attention to her.

Nor did he leave her in any doubt about the honor of his intentions. The chaos of law in Texas was to their advantage, he explained, for when she and Solomon Page had entered Texas it was under Mexican rule and according to law any couple had to be remarried by a priest for legality. Page had neglected that among the many other failures of his responsibility. Technically, therefore, their marriage was null and void, and Harriet was free to marry again. When the new laws for the new Republic would be written, Robert Potter would be among those who would write them for such contingencies, so she should have no cause to worry about her status, not as Mrs. Robert Potter.

Harriet had planned to go to Kentucky with her son when she could. Her grandmother was there and a decent life, however lonely, was possible. But now she loved Robert Potter and she trusted him. Even so, she waited and made him wait.

Then word came of Sam Houston's startling victory at San Jacinto and the capture of Santa Anna. At once Potter went with the other officials to conclude matters. He and Burnet and Lamar were against any treaty. They insisted that the Mexican general be executed, and their admiration of the wounded Houston was grudging. The fact that Houston opposed their wishes and dealt the treaty according to his own judgment only widened the breach in politics for the new government.

Potter returned to Galveston and sailed his ship with Harriet to New Orleans. Then, instead of going up the Mississippi to Kentucky and Harriet's grandmother, he navigated up the Red River into northeast Texas. No woman was ever abducted more romantically nor with greater chivalry and irresistible determination.

Their marriage bond and contract was signed September 5 with three witnesses, and their destination was a home of rare rustic beauty on the land Potter had claimed on the lakes of the Caddo Indians—the Ferry and Sodo Lakes, as they were known then in the great pine forests of northeast Texas, Red River County.

The year 1836 had seen a new nation born and a new life for this man and woman at home at Potter's Point.

Meanwhile, in a parallel of time, the story of another North Carolinian was unfolding in a very different way, and yet a way which also led into this orbit of new country.

His name was William Pinckney Rose, and he was born in Oxford, North Carolina, in the spring of 1787. His was a family of distinction, for his mother was a niece of George Washington and his father John Rose was an officer in the Revolutionary War.

The Roses moved to Georgia, and from there William went to Louisiana and into the army of General Andrew Jackson.

He came out of the Battle of New Orleans a captain. In 1816 he married a young widow, Mrs. Mary Vardaman Smith, and after seven years of plantation life in Louisiana, Captain Rose moved his family to a plantation in Mississippi. There he became a member of the Constitutional Convention and later the legislature. He was a man respected for both his physical and political fearlessness.

Over six feet tall and heavily muscular, Captain Rose commanded obedience, especially from his nine children. After his move to Texas in 1839, it was not by chance that he was referred to as "Hell-roarin' Rose" and "The Lion of the Lakes" in Red River County.

For such men as Captain Rose and Colonel Potter to become neighbors was a trick of fate which could only spell trouble. Each man was a law unto himself, and ironically enough, they first met in a court of law that day in March, 1840, in Clarksville when Potter decided to begin practice again as adjunct to his political career.

Several of Potter's former associates from the hectic time at Washington-on-the-Brazos were in the Clarksville courthouse that day, men such as Mr. Collin McKinney, Mr. Richard Ellis, and Mr. Albert Latimer. They introduced him to Captain Rose, well aware that this contact of giant personalities would generate some interesting events sooner or later.

For a year Rose and Potter were friendly, but in 1841 conflict began with much of it sparked by the feud known as the Regulator-Moderator War.

Capt. Rose was a Regulator who believed that the cause of justice should be adminstered privately with a man's own gun. Potter, who by paradox had always taken the law into his own hands in the past, was now on the side of law and accordingly was a member of the Moderator faction.

Potter had already won election to the Senate over Mr. John Denton, who was supported by Rose. When Rose and his associates were indicted by a Red River County grand

jury for murdering a sheriff and two other men, there was a
change of venue to Harrison County. Potter persuaded President Mirabeau B. Lamar to offer a reward of five hundred
dollars for Rose's capture, and Senator Potter announced that
he would personally go to arrest him and bring him to trial.

The Sixth Congress in Austin had adjourned in early February, 1842, and Potter had returned home at once. He was
tired from the long and busy session, his work as chairman
of the Public Lands Committee, the effort it had taken to pass
the measure to establish Marshall University, and all the social
affairs connected with the inauguration of President Sam
Houston. But he took no time to rest. He brushed aside Harriet's fears for him and went to make good his promise to
arrest Rose.

So much was written about what happened then, not only
in Texas but also in the United States and even abroad in
England, and so much of what was written was distorted and
disputed that perhaps the best source to quote first is the
diary of Mrs. Potter, who shared and witnessed that finale.

It was early in March when my husband brought the President's
proclamation down to the Point, and gathered a company of seventeen men to assist in capturing this outlaw. In those days Texas
was ruled by two parties, the moderators and regulators; the former believed in administering justice in a legal way and the latter
dealing it out in arbitrary and usually quite sudden fashion. Col.
Potter belonged to the moderator's party and Old Rose was to be
imprisoned and tried by law in the County courthouse.

Old Rose was busily engaged in supervising the work of his
negroes who were clearing off a piece of ground and burning the
brush-wood upon it, piling the brush in heaps and then setting
fire to it, when he saw a number of men riding towards his house.
He realized that he was outnumbered and knew well what their
visit portended, so down he fell upon the ground and ordered the
negroes to pile brushwood over him at once. He knew that Col.
Potter had offered to plead against him when he was captured,
and that at his request President Lamar would take effective steps
towards his arrest.

The men were all armed when they rode up to Rose's house and presented their warrant, for they intended to overpower their prisoner and take him without blood-shed if possible. He was not there however, nor could they find him anywhere upon the place. It did not occur to them to look under the brushwood piles for him.

Preston Rose was a nice young man who had just married a short while before this event; he was not at all like his father, and so, when they failed to find the old man he begged my husband to go peaceably away, that he would make his father give himself up and be tried. Col. Potter believed him, the more readily perhaps, because he was tired out from his long trip to Austin. Preston assured my husband that if his father refused to go peacefully or if there was any danger to him or the men with him on account of this visit that he would notify us so that we might be prepared.

Satisfied that Old Rose would give himself up without further trouble, the men dispersed and my husband came home. "When Old Rose hears that you have been hunting for him he will come tonight and try to kill you," I said. I begged him to gather all the men he could and have them in the house with firearms ready for an attack, but he only laughed at my fears. He admitted that Rose might feel revengeful, but that it would be impossible for him to get men enough that night to make an attack. He was so tired that he would not listen to any thought of danger, and so went to rest.

When darkness had settled down over the forest and the angel of Peace had brought sleep to weary eyes, evil spirits were going to and fro plotting murder. Old Rose felt sure that if he would compass Col. Potter's death no one else would dare to molest him. I felt very anxious as night advanced, and presently the barking of dogs warned me that some stranger was around our home.

I woke my husband up and called his attention to this fact, but he would not believe that the house was being surrounded and said that he was very tired and to let him alone. I was too uneasy to sleep any myself and listened intently to the sounds outside; the barking and growling of dogs, the whirr of the crickets in the woods, and I could almost imagine the foot-falls of human beings.

So the night wore on until I felt that I could bear the suspense no longer. We always had our meal ground for breakfast in a steel mill, and it was almost time for the performance of that first morning duty. I arose and woke the boy whose business it was to grind the meal, and told him it was time to get the meal ready for breakfast. The boy was obliged to cross the yard in order to reach the corn crib and get a supply of corn for the mill. In a few moments he went out; he did not return, and as time went on the gray morning began to break into the dusk of night and shadows became less deep and dark, I roused my brother and told him about the boy's absence. He went out to look for him, and he, too, remained. We had an old man living with us who always fed the hogs and when he started to go out to his work I said to him, "It is very strange that George does not commence to grind the meal for breakfast. I wish you would see what is the matter." I waited awhile, and unable to stand the anxiety any longer I decided to go myself.

I stepped out into the early morning and started toward the kitchen. Just as the man Hezekiah went over the stile some little distance from the left hand side of the house, I was halfway to the kitchen. A posse shot him down and tried to take me prisoner. I was very active and darted away from them and ran into the house. Several shots were fired and their sound awoke my husband.

"What does that mean?" he asked me, as I came into the house.

"It means that the house is surrounded, and that we will have to fight or die," I replied.

"Where are all the men?" he inquired, at once on the alert.

Then I said what I always regretted saying, for I think it was a terrible blow to him, that probably discouraged him from making any defense. "I suppose the men are all killed; they have just killed one," I answered.

Then he wanted to escape from the house, but I begged him not to go, and our little daughter whom he loved tenderly, cried and screamed for her Papa not to leave her. I think he was unnerved by the loss of the men and thought that his only safety lay in getting away from the house.

He looked through a small crack in the wall at the back of the house and seeing the number of the attacking party he said that the only thing for him to do was to get down to the lake where he would be safe as he was a fine swimmer. We had a cannon and plenty of firearms all loaded, and I reminded him that I could load guns as fast as he could.

"We can defend ourselves," I said. "I will stand by you as long as we both live. If you will just kill Old Rose and Scott the difficulty will be at an end." But in the haste and excitement of the moment he paid no attention to the argument.

As he left the house he said, "They cannot hurt you anyhow." He ran from the house and jumped the fence. Just by the fence stood Sandy Miller and Stephen Peters. "Why, these are my friends," he called out to me. "No, they are not friends," I answered back, and as he jumped over the rails both men fired at him. The group who had been stationed behind the house yelled like Indians as they fired after Col. Potter's retreating form, and pointed the way he had gone.

He ran down the hill and along the beach under the cliff, unhurt by the bullets which whistled after him. We had cut steps down the steep bank to the spring and at the foot of these grew three magnificent cypress trees. Leaning his gun against one of these trees my husband sprang into the lake and dived out of sight of his pursuers. Scott ran down the bank behind him, while Old Rose levelled his gun at me and ordered me to go into the house.

What careless spirit could have entered my husband's mind and caused him to leave his gun on the shore is more than I could ever comprehend. Scott seized it, and as Col. Potter's head rose out of the lake he fired. Old Rose, still with his gun drawn on me, tried to force me to go in, but I told him that I would not move a step, nor did I.

Presently Scott came up the bank and said to Rose, with some indignation, "What are you abusing Mrs. Potter for? She has never done you any harm. Come on, let's go, we have done what we came to do." I thought they were just talking to annoy me, now that my husband had escaped them. Our small cannon loaded with buckshot stood beside me, but I had been unable to find the matches to fire it with.

The other men released the boy and my brother whom they had taken prisoners, and I went with George to see if Hezekiah was quite dead. We found him living and dressed his wounds from which he finally recovered. When Hezekiah had been cared for, we began to look for Col. Potter.

He was not on the islands nor on the shore. We searched all that day for him until I despaired of even finding him alive and thought that, after all, Scott had killed him when he fired into the lake with his gun.

How horrible that broad sheet of water seemed to me, who had once thought it so beautiful. What dreadful secret did it hold from me? That night, as if all the elements were in sympathy with my tortured mind, there was a terrible thunderstorm. In the morning we decided to take the cannon down to the lake and fire it across the water so that if Col. Potter had indeed been drowned we might recover his body. We had rowed about the lake all day before, searching it well with a large spyglass, and nothing else was left for us to do.

We got the cannon down to the place from which he had jumped into the lake, for his tracks were plainly visible, but there was no need to fire it, for there in the early morning light my husband lay asleep upon the water. That was a terrible time for me; we carried him up to the house and found that he had been shot in the back of his head. In his trousers pocket was the match I had needed so sorely to fire the cannon upon his murderers.

There were only two among all the men who he had befriended who dared to come and help bury him. There was a beautiful knoll on the hill in front of the house where a clump of tall trees grew. My husband had often said that when he died he would like to be buried there. So we bore his body to the grave beneath the clump of trees that he had loved, and laid it there to rest . . .[2]

Capt. Rose died nine years later (in 1851), and it is of interest to note that when he died he requested to be buried with friends in Marshall. Not his family. Evidently he went to his reward still a Regulator.

The impact of all the tragedy, however, fell upon Harriet, for when Robert Potter's will was read, the husband she loved and whose murder she was determined to avenge had dealt her a blow of betrayal which few women could survive. He did not claim her as his wife, but referred to her by the name of Harriet *Page,* and he named two other women prominent in Austin society to share in the estate.

But even this mystery and scandal she faced and endured with all the strength of her memories of happiness with him and with the children of that happiness. In her heart there were no doubts and no questions. In her mind, yes, but not in her heart.

Moreover, the future held another man to restore her faith in love. His name was Charles Ames, and as Mrs. Charles Ames she was to live into an old age of fulfillment as matriarch of children and grandchildren of honor as Texans and Americans.

---

[2]In October 1928 Robert Potter's coffin was exhumed and removed to the State Cemetery in Austin with a monument erected at the grave.

To visit Potter's Point today and see the vast expanse of lake (seventy-five square miles) with the wild ducks afloat among the dark cypress trunks is still to sense a wilderness, to hear a strange silence which whispers of violence, however softly.

No markers are there. Only a sign six miles away pointing toward the lake. And there is always someone along the road who says, "You know why that's called Potter's Point? Ole Mrs. ——— she can tell you when they played a bugle and dug up his grave. And there's a book about him too . . ."

21.

The Hanging Tree

IN the old Clarksville cemetery stands an ancient oak tree which has been a name of awesome distinction since the year 1837.

Variously called "Page's Tree" or "The Hanging Tree," its public utility of sorts began when several slaves ran away from the plantations of Capt. Charlie Burkham and Levi Davis. The Negroes were traced to the Sabine River but were never found. Riding home again, Burkham and Davis stopped at the farmhouse of a man named Page and were never heard of again.

After a few days their families and friends set out to find them and saw a man riding a mule which they recognized as one of Burkham's. The fellow said he had bought it from Page. They hurried there and took Page, his son and son-in-law and a Mexican into custody, as the Mexican and Page's son confessed the murder.

A vigilance committee held a "trial" and used this tree to hang them all. From then on, the tree served the cause of "justice."

Late in 1837 when the Red River region was in dispute between the Republic of Texas and the Arkansas Territory of the United States, the people of this region decided very definitely in favor of the Republic of Texas which so far had levied no taxes. The Territory of Arkansas was collecting all the money possible and sent the sheriff of Miller County, Arkansas, to Clarksville to collect what he could there. Instead, his reception committee escorted him out to Page's Tree and explained its purpose and rather forcibly suggested that he leave at once or become its next decoration. Taking the committee at their word, the sheriff made haste for the Arkansas line.

In an interview for the *Clarksville News* in 1899, Capt. J. B. Donoho, whose father had been one of the Santa Fe traders, reported that as a boy in the late 1830's he used to ride behind his father on horseback past the tree, and "I remember having seen three men hung there by what used to be the old Baptist cemetery."

More about the tree is in the record of an 1841 lawsuit filed by a John Boon against six men who bound and took him to Page's Tree, tied him to it and beat him.

Another case is recalled in the memoirs of Capt. James Clark concerning a horse thief who was captured and taken to Page's Tree. Quite an audience gathered to watch the procedure, including a number of ladies. Since there was no jail, something had to be done with the man. But Capt. Clark's stepfather Dr. George Gordon made an eloquent speech for mercy and suggested a vote to be taken on whether the thief should be hanged or set free. He also pled that the ladies be allowed to vote, and finally after much argument the men agreed to let the women have this unheard-of privilege. As result and by this narrow female margin, the vote set the man free.

Years later Capt. Clark was in a certain town in Mississippi on legal business and he was introduced to a leading citizen who immediately asked him if he happened to know Dr.

Gordon of Clarksville. When Clark explained their relation-
ship, the gentleman asked him to deliver a message of gratitude
to the doctor for having saved him from hanging on the big
branch of Page's Tree. The act of mercy had reformed him for
life.

In an 1885 interview for a Weatherford, Texas, newspaper,
Mrs. C. E. Carey recalled, "I have seen the self-constituted
authorities pass my door in Clarksville with many victims of
Page's Tree fifty years ago."

In the summer of 1959 when a representative of the Inter-
national Paper Co., Mr. E. R. Mueller, was in Clarksville, he
was asked to examine the historic tree and estimate its age.
His figure was 216 years.

The birds nest in its branches comfortably now, and the
many squirrels store their acorns against the winter months.
Only a handful of the descendants of Old Red River families
who handed down its story point it out in awe as once did the
men and women who now rest in the old cemetery beneath its
shade.

22.

A Bit of Bigamy

IN the early spring of the year 1840 when a steamboat landed at the Red River port of Rowland, among the passengers who came down the gangplank to stand on Texas soil for the first time were a man and woman with two children in their arms, and they spoke with such a strange accent that everyone stared at them.

To Rowland Bryarly, founder of the little port town who was always on hand to welcome newcomers, the man introduced himself as John Monkhouse and the woman as his wife Ann. They had come from England, he explained, to seek their fortune in the future of this new frontier.

At once Bryarly arranged for lodging for them and assured Monkhouse that his fortune could be made right here in Rowland. In a few days' time the handsome Englishman agreed with him, for with the Indians eager for trade across the river, and with the steamboat crews thirsting for refreshment, the opportunity for a good tavern here was obvious. Besides, Ann Monkhouse had been a barmaid in England and she knew the business. And so a "pub" was opened on a river as far removed from the Thames as one could be.

Business was good. In exchange for whiskey, the Monkhouses took vast quantities of hides and furs from the Choctaws, as well as the snakeroot and pinkroot which had steady sale to drug companies in the East through New Orleans.

All went well, very well, until early in the year 1847 when a lady arrived in nearby Clarksville. He name was also Mrs. John Monkhouse, and she had come from England to claim her legal rights as his wife and the mother of his six children.

Instead, there began one of those stories of quietly endured sacrifice and devotion which some women are capable of, as Mary Monkhouse was. When she learned about Ann Monkhouse and of John's happiness with her and *their* children, and when she learned too about all that would be involved in such a case if she pressed her claim, Mary decided not to ruin the home which he had created in Rowland. She withdrew herself socially and went to work as housekeeper for a Mrs. Isabella Gordon in Clarksville.

If Mary Monkhouse ever met her husband and Ann across the few miles which separated the little towns, there is no record of such a triangle tryst.

John, however, showed no appreciation of his wife's gesture. On the contrary, he ruthlessly took action to show where his heart lay, for on May 18, 1847, he made a deed of gift to Ann Edmondson, alias Ann Monkhouse, and their children Margaret, William, James, Henry, and Charlotte. This deed included "one negro man Peter, one negro woman Easter, 3 horses, 2 mules, 80 head cattle, all household and kitchen goods, stock of merchandise, all notes and accounts, 50 hogs, 2 wagons, 150 acres land, 7 town lots in Town of Rowland."

Obviously he had prospered in his seven years in Rowland. In addition, he had a public warehouse and was a customs agent for the Republic of Texas.

But John Monkhouse did not live long to enjoy this success, for in another two years he died of malaria. The tombstone erected by his barmaid "wife" in the Rowland cemetery still presents a legible inscription after well over a century.

In Memory of John Monkhouse
Born Jan. 9, 1792
Died Oct. , 1849
Farewell Dear Wife and Children Dear,
I am not gone but sleeping here,
As I lie mouldering in the dust,
Until the Resurrection of the Just.

Before Monkhouse began his wait for heavenly approval, the records show that he and his old friend Bryarly had parted company and kept the courts busy with lawsuits against each other, which finally some of their heirs had to settle as late as 1870.

When Ann Monkhouse took over her late "husband's" property and business, gossip ran higher than the river's tide. But she was determined to protect her children and take her place in "a man's world." Soon, however, her own lawsuits began piling up (twenty-three cases in all), and they were more often as defendant than plaintiff with other merchants, New Orleans cotton factors and commission men, and steamboat captains.

By the time she died in early December, 1863, she had lost everything. Of course, almost everyone else in the Confederate States was reduced to the same poverty by then, as the fateful reports drifted across the country from Gettysburg and Vicksburg.

The first and legally rightful Mrs. John Monkhouse (Mary) had died seven years earlier without ever having pressed her claim. Of her thoughts and feelings no record exists. Certainly she could have supplied any Victorian novelist or poet with her story of girlhood romance and elopement and then the disillusionment and loneliness of a woman deserted and betrayed. Yet she had preserved some inner pride and integrity which remained inviolate.

More than a hint of this is implied in a letter of April 19, 1957, from her great-great-granddaughter Edith Cruttenden in Sussex, England: "John Monkhouse was a butler to the Faulkners at Witham Hall, Lincoln, England. He eloped with one of the daughters, Mary Faulkner, but was caught in London and married at Old St. Pancras Church. He went to America between 1835 and 1840, leaving his wife and family (six children) . . . A letter my mother had which he wrote in April 1846 from Clarksville, Rowland, Red River, Texas, U.S.A., asking his daughter Hannah Maria (my grandmother) to go out to him. . . . (they) found a woman posing as his wife and some children. His wife was staying with a Dr. and Mrs. Gordon . . . But my mother said her mother and aunt did not want to be any bother to anyone and it would only mean a lot of letters to write about property . . . "

If those letters had been written by the hesitant ladies who were his legitimate heirs, there would have been another and very different story along the river and also across the sea.

23.

River Voyages

F ROM what remains of a diary written by an Irish Presbyterian minister named John Anderson comes a simple but
graphic account of what it meant to travel on the rivers from
Virginia to the Texas frontier in 1844.

Rev. Anderson had come with his wife from County
Tyrone in Ireland to Fincastle, Botetourt County, Virginia,
where they taught school until the glowing reports of the new
country to the west made him restless enough to venture the
trip and see if it might be safe for a woman and children.

He began the diary in September 1844 and ended it
abruptly a month later on the White River in Arkansas, still
a considerable distance from his destination.

* * *

Left Fincastle at 3½ A.M. and shortly after got a sulky
horse which refused to move forward. When the stage was
nearly upset the horse was loosed from the stage and taken
back for a mile and half and another one obtained (raining
all the time we were delayed).

We arrived at the commencement of the salt works buildings at a little after 5 o'clock. We stopped and visited one of the establishments in full operation. The number of salt establishments in operation is immense. The river after the junction of the Ganley and the New River is beautiful. We passed by the Hawks Nest (or as it is known in history by the name of Marshall's Pillar) 1010 feet perpendicular over the bank of the New River about 9 o'clock. The Falls of the Kanawha are where the river runs over a number of beds of sandstone and the falls are not more than 9 or 10 feet high. The water being low and the falls not at right angles to the running water, but rather on the inside and then running through openings, making little noise. Arrived at Charleston at 8 P.M. Found a stage to start in the morning at 7½ A.M. for Guyandotte and though unwilling to travel on Sunday ascertained that we would not get a boat from Guyandotte until Tuesday or Wednesday and perhaps not then, so we decided to try for the boat for Monday Morning.

Sunday, September 29th

Left Charleston for Guyandotte at 7½ after spending a tolerably comfortable night. There I found mosquito bars on the beds. Before retiring to rest I committed myself to the care of my Covenant-keeping God and praying for his blessing to rest on my dear family.

Arrived at Black's Tavern at 3½ P.M. where we dined and started for Guyandotte. Arrived at Guyandotte where we found several passengers waiting for a boat, but no chance of getting one probably for a day or two and then only a chance of getting a very small one, where we will not have more than sufficient room to stand on deck. The fare also to Cincinnati is considerably raised, advantage being taken of the lowness of the water. Went on board at 10.

Monday, September 30th

No appearance of a boat this morning and the Ohio is so low, that it can easily be forded, opposite to this. Two boats passed down yesterday one of which stuck fast on the bar for several hours but finally got off leaving many passengers here who wanted to go on south. I hope we may soon have a boat, as I do not like this hotel, though the people are civil, but the accommodations are indifferent.

Went at 7½ A.M. to a meeting of a Clay Club and heard a speech in favor of Clay and just as a second speaker commenced I got word that a boat was in sight. I left the Club and got on the *Belfast* with the aid of a cane and thought we would start immediately after for Cincinnati. After we got on board made inquiry for a berth—and got none—tried for a mattress—all were occupied with 5 or 6 gentlemen and four ladies. Had to sit up all night in the cabin.

Tuesday, October 1st

Got under way this morning, at 7½ o'clock. Those lying on the floor of the cabin were called at 3½ o'clock. They were much enraged at being roused up so early. There was scarcely room enough for the passengers to stand in the cabin. Eating on this boat is most miserable. Spent a miserable day. Often did I wish I was with my dear family. After supper I laid hold of a mattress determined at last to make provision for sleeping. I laid it down on the floor but could scarcely sleep. I arose about 4½ and found that my right ankle or rather a little above it was swollen considerably and a dark red spot the size of a silver dollar 1½ inches above the ankle was sore to the touch. I was thankful for the little sleep I got and that our boat, though it had bad accommodations, did not get aground as others.

Wednesday, October 2nd

Nothing worthy of incident occurred this day. I passed one town with more than 100 Clay flags erected (Maysville I believe). We arrived at Cincinnati at 2 P.M. and went to the —————————House, a very excellent hotel. Here we heard that the river was so low no boats could start from here further down than Louisville. We walked through the city for several hours and were much pleased with its appearance. Having lost my hat overboard on Tuesday, I had to buy a cap at Portsmouth and here I purchased a hat for $5.00.

I engaged my passage to Louisville on board the *Plymouth* for $3 to sail tomorrow at 10 o'clock. Returned to rest feeling grateful to God for his goodness.

Thursday, October 3rd

Left Cincinnati at 11 A.M. on board the *Plymouth*. An excellent boat and excellent servants on board. I passed the day mostly reading when I could fix my attention on what I was reading.

We arrived at Louisville on Friday morning at 4 o'clock at sunrise, went to the Galt House which was full of company. Here I learned that the Canal [1] was closed and would not be opened for from 5 to 15 days. Engaged a carriage after breakfast for $1 to take us below the mouth of the canal. We found 3 boats for the mouth of the Ohio 400 miles away, and though all were advertised to sail this day, we soon ascertained that but one would sail and that she would charge whatever passage money she chose. We engaged our passage to sleep on the cabin floor for 15 dollars on board the *Lucy Long* to sail at 4 P.M.

Friday, October 4th

Arrived at Portland at the mouth of the canal and got on board the *Lucy Long* at 11 o'clock. She is to sail at 4 P.M. We found the boat crowded and many pasengers who came from Louisville to sail by her had to return. We started at 4 and got on pretty well till about 4 in the morning. No incident

---

[1]This was the canal at the Falls of the Ohio at Louisville. It was then known as the Louisville and Portland Canal. It was built by a private company with the United States as one of the stockholders and opened in 1830 with a lift of 8 2/3 feet. From 1860 to 1872 the canal was much enlarged and improved, and in 1874 the United States Government became the sole owner.

worthy of mention occurred during the day. Louisville is a dirty-looking place, but I was through very little of it as we did not remain but a few hours.

On board the *Lucy Long* we found many of our fellow travelers from Guyandotte. Every place is crowded with passengers and their baggage, and we will only get room on a little mattress to sleep on. The time hangs very heavily on our hands as from the confusion on board it is impossible to read. I have not had one hour's comfortable sleep since I left home nor do I expect to do so until I get to Memphis. I thank God that my health is as good as can be, though the water, tea, and coffee are miserable.

Since I came on board the boat at Guyandotte, I am not certain I have met any professor of religion. Almost all play cards and use profane language, and I have not met more than 3 or 4 members of temperance societies. I am determined to be faithful to my pledge.

Saturday, October 5th

In consequence of a very heavy fog on the river we did not start this morning until near 9 o'clock. We got fast on a sand bar where we were kept 4 hours. Started off the sand bar and again got aground on Anderson's Bar where another vessel is fast as we are.

Sunday, October 6th

Last night captain and some hands went ashore to get some wood. After they had cut down a couple and brought them to the shore, they found that their boat had been stolen. They finally found it with the other steamboat lying on the bar. Our Captain threw the man who stole the boat overboard and left him to get ashore as best he could.

Got up at 5 this morning. It was cold and wet. I am much afraid that this will not be a pleasant Sabbath.

2 o'clock—all has been bustle and discomfort this day. The

boat has just got over the bar. The gentlemen passengers had to remain 5 hours on board a flat to lighten the boat. There was no place to sit but some empty barrels.

4 o'clock—We dined comfortably and are now getting along well. People are talking politics all around me, and were I to judge the election of Clay from the number of his adherants on board, I suppose Clay would be elected. I have heard no Democrat who pretends to argue the subject under dispute. I have engaged in religious conversation a little on several occasions with different persons, but they do not seem to relish what I said.

7 P.M.—We are hard and fast on a bar and there is little prospect of our getting off before morning. Oh! the miserable night which is before me. Lying on a straw mattress in the cabin, with the engines and kicking horses below. I do not expect to sleep 20 minutes in succession.

1½ A.M.—We have just got off the bar and sailed about a couple of miles and now will cast anchor for the night as the Three Mile Bar is just ahead of us. I did not sleep 10 minutes from the time I went to bed until I got up at 1 A.M. They are as industrious as possible (I mean the captain and the crew).

Monday, October 7th

I again went to bed at 2. The boat struck against shoal bars but we finally anchored just above the 3 mile bar.

6½ A.M.—We have just started and are doing well.

7 A.M.—Hard and fast on a bar. We got off in almost an hour.

10 P.M.—This has been the most incessant day's talking of politics I ever heard. The ladies on both sides are perfectly rabid. A vote was taken on board and in the cabin. There were 27 Whigs and 14 Democrats. The vote was taken in the steerage and there were, including the hands, 16 Democrats and 6 Whigs. The vote stood, without ladies and children at 33 Whigs and 30 Democrats.

We have gotten along well all day and are now fast approaching ———— 80 miles from the mouth. The days are miserably long, the accommodations for sleeping are so bad no person can enjoy comfort.

Tuesday, October 8th

We lay above the bar called The Three Sisters from 3 o'clock till 8½ A.M. The fog was exceedingly dense this morning so that we could not make an early start. The nights have been very cold ever since I left home. The weather is still very dry, no rain having fallen for several weeks. The river is very beautiful, a tolerably clear river with high banks. The villages of which there are many on the shore do not generally look very good.

9 A.M.—We have just arrived at the mouth of the Ohio and taken our passage on board the *Champlain,* which sails in the morning for New Orleans. She seems to be a very fine vessel, large and roomy with excellent accommodations.

About 4 o'clock this afternoon I had some very sharp conversation with a gentleman by the name of Miner from New Orleans. I found out afterwards that he was a very ignorant man, who had been left by the death of an uncle $250,000 about 4 years ago. Nearly all my fellow passengers were delighted that I took him down so.

I got a berth with some difficulty when I came on the *Champlain* and anticipate a good night's rest. May an allwise Providence guard and protect my dear wife and children and grant us a happy meeting when I return to Fincastle.

Wednesday, October 9th

We got up early this morning, and I walked a little on the Illinois shore. Cairo has but one hotel and two or three miserable-looking houses. We started for Memphis (242 miles) at 10 minutes before 7 and at 9½ passed Mills Point 40 miles from the mouth of the Ohio.

10 P.M.—We made a run of about 140 miles this day until

7 and then lay to for the night. The fare on board is very bad. Nothing worthy of notice this day.

Thursday, October 10th

We made an early start this morning as the river was free from fog. We had scarcely half food set before us at breakfast and when I looked at the dinner table it was enough for me.

We arrived at Memphis at 3 P.M. and had our trunks left at the Central Hotel, a most miserable place. I called soon after my arrival on Doctor Shanks who was extremely glad to see me and brought me to his house and sent for my trunks to the hotel. Mr. Gray had to go to Holly Springs. I will probably remain here for a couple of days perhaps after Sunday. I intend to write three letters, one to my dear wife and one to Major Pryor and one to Mr. Bradshaw. I anticipate a good night's rest, an enjoyment of which I have been deprived since I left home. God preserve me and mine.

Thursday, October 17th

12 Noon—I have just started for the mouth of the White River (175) miles). When I came here last Thursday, I had just 12 dollars and 25 cents. Mr. Gray has only 2 dollars. I lent him money to carry him to Holly Springs 50 miles from Memphis, where he expected to get money from Doctor Carruthers there. He had an account to collect from Mr. Archibald Walker at Memphis. He could not get it and he started on Saturday for Holly Springs. He returned on Monday at 6 P.M. and did not get a cent. He was promised Walker's account on Wednesday, 35 dollars which, had he got them, would have brought him to the end of his journey. He was disappointed, and consequently I had to leave him behind. I borrowed 30 dollars from Doctor Shanks. I was during my stay at his house treated with utmost hospitality.

I left his house yesterday afternoon at 5 P.M. and expected to sail immediately, but it having commenced to rain with a heavy thundershower, the boat did not start till 12. There seem to be about 70 passengers on board and at least 2000 bales of cotton. The boat is called the *Eclipse,* a very fast and comfortable boat.

I preached on Sunday forenoon and night at the Presbyterian Church to a very large congregation. The pastor Mr. C———— was absent attending Presbytery. I trust my labors may not be in vain. The audience was very attentive.

I have been laid up with rheumatism in my right ankle and knee in Memphis. I applied medicine which Doctor Shanks recommended, and I am now, thank God, quite well. Still I am afraid to put on my boots. I do not like Memphis. Half the city seemed unoccupied. The business is confined to a small portion of the city. The dust was several inches deep when I came to it, but several showers laid the dust and changed it into mud of an equal depth.

Friday, October 18th

We arrived at the mouth of the White River at 4 P.M. The *Eclipse* sailed fast. We found that the mail boat would arrive in about 2 hours, and as the postmaster, Mr. Williams, from Little Rock, was wanting to return, he stated one should start immediately after the arrival of the mail boat. The Mississippi presented the same monotonous appearance down to the mouth of the White River. Here and there a few scattering houses and a few acres of land partially cleared, but presenting the appearance of wretchedness and poverty. The sickly looks of those engaged in the healthy exercise of wood clearing proclaimed in language not to be misinterpreted the general unhealthy state of the country.

We had our luggage left on the wharf boat and went to the Hotel Montgomery, where we supped heavily for the second time since leaving Fincastle. 37½ cents for the meal. The hotel, the Purple Monty, is the picture of wretchedness. The barkeeper in conversation with our party for Little Rock said, "Oh, that I had just one sight of Kentucky, it would make me well."

After supper we went on the mail boat, the *Birksville,* a miserable, uncomfortable little tub—filthy low cabin, dirty beds and as for cooking ————enough!

We started about 9 P.M. and about 11 took wood. After taking in wood on the White River, the Captain and the crew could not get the boat off a log on which it had settled. The boat draws but 15 inches of water.

* * *

Evidently the rest of the diary was lost, but the result of the trip, despite its discomforts, was to convince the teacher-preacher that he could return home and bring his family westward where they could hold their own against the non-Presbyterians.

He moved them to Clarksville and by 1850 had established himself teaching school and performing marriage and funeral ceremonies on the side for families favoring ritual flavored with Irish brogue. Obviously there were enough of the latter so that he could afford to acquire some property.

In fact, in the fall of 1865 he was able to embark on another trip, this time all the way to New York as well as to his old home in Ireland. Though this diary fragment reports the trip only as far as Illinois, several post-Civil War observations are of special interest in addition to the daily adventures of river travel.

* * *

Left Clarksville and arrived at Jefferson on the morn of 24th October. Friday: went on board the *Lizzie Hamilton* and paid $10.00 passage to Shreveport, then found she will not sail till Saturday evening. Went on board the *Sciene No. 2.* Was told she would sail on Friday evening. She did not start until Saturday night and then only got as far as the packery. Started on Sunday morning, took on more freight—already had about 300 bales of cotton. Made about 12 miles on Sunday and about 20 during the night.

Monday, October 30th

Found we had lost a rudder during the night. At 8 A.M. just entering the lakes—a passenger shot a large alligator. Caught on a stump and laid there all night and the next two days at the entrance of Soda Lake.

November, 1st

Got under way about 7¼ P.M. and are now about 30 miles from Shreveport. Will get there some time this day. The *Lizzie Hamilton* passed us at 8¼ A.M. Arrived at Shreveport at 3 P.M. commenced taking on cotton. Took about 100 bales. Left Shreveport at night.

November, 2nd

Started from Shreveport at 3½ P.M. with a cargo of 529 bales of cotton and went on for 45 miles and laid up all night. The weather cold and gloomy with some rain nearly all the time.

November, 3rd

Started at 5 A.M., the weather still gloomy. We are getting on well. We have about 30 passengers. We have a chess board and some good players. I have not tried whether I can beat them, but intend trying this day. Got on a bar and stayed all night.

Saturday, November 4th

Made about 14 miles in the morning and got on a log or stump which punched a hole in the boat about 18 inches from the keel. No alarm—the carpenters were at work all day and got the boat ready for sailing about 11 P.M.

Played chess with the two best players and beat both in succession—5 games to 2 each. Several others wanted me to play, but I declined playing except with the best.

Got under way this morning at daylight—a fine day. The

river is very low—from 3½ to 5 feet of water on the bars. Have to haul over all the bars.

I played chess with best two players, beat one three games but the other got two to my one. Dinner bell will ring in a few minutes. It is said if we do not get on better we will be on short allowance.

Sunday Morn.—After sailing nearly 2 weeks yesterday, got fast on a bar where we stayed all day and last night. During the night we put off about 100 bales of cotton to enable the boat to get down the river. While trying to get the boat off we broke 5 teeth out of the wheel of the niggerhead and could go no further.

This evening we got off and are getting along slowly and safely. Everything on board is very quiet. There were 2 big fights between the negro hands on board yesterday.

Monday, November 6th
Got on a bar after two hours sail and remained there all afternoon.

Tuesday, November 7th
Got off the bar about 12 at night and laid to till morning. Found two arms of the stern wheel broken and are repairing. Little likelihood that we will get away from here this forenoon. And we are about 20 to 25 miles above Campi. If a boat from above comes along I intend to get off this and try another. I expected to be at New Orleans this morning.

At 10 A.M. the *David Watts* came which left Shreveport on Saturday. I induced 4 other passengers to quit the *Sciene No. 2*. At 12 noon we are getting along and will have passed Campi in about 1 hour. About ½ mile below we passed the *Glide* sunk and all her cotton strewed along the banks, having been taken out of the water. Are still passing cotton lodged in the river. We will soon be at Grand Ecore. I hope we will be in New Orleans on Thursday morning.

Tuesday Night, 7 P.M.—We arrived within one mile of Grand Ecore and got on a bar with only 22 inches of water. We tried to get off from 3 P.M. until this time. We are nearly over. I believe this is the worst bar to New Orleans.

While we were trying to cross, the *Caddo,* which left Shreveport on Saturday last, passed us without difficulty. I think we will make good speed tomorrow. I do not think the *Sciene No. 2* will get here in a week. I am well pleased with the change. I was sorry to leave the *Sciene* as the passengers were generally very nice people. I do not think much of the passengers here. Several very plain ladies of a certain age are on board who evidently might have been married before the war.

Wednesday, November 8th

Got on a bar within a mile of Grand Ecore at 4 P.M. and did not get off till 1 A.M. Then went a little below Grand Ecore, took on 63 bales of cotton. Up this morn at 5 and went to see the old fort. Nothing remarkable to see. A few soldiers in the place. I forgot to state that at the bar where we were so long detained on Monday, we went on shore and saw the battlefield where General Green was killed and where Gould's regiment did good service.[2] At 10 A.M. we got on a log and are still there trying to get off. The *Sciene* I think will overtake us. We took on board just before getting on the log 22 more bales of cotton—we now have too much—now we will probably have to work over every sand bar until we come to the Mississippi. 12 noon and still on the log. It is truly monotonous. Here I am 100 miles from Alexandria. Got off at 3 and stopped at 4 to take on 25 bales of cotton. Stopped at about 6 miles and took in some wood and laid up for the night.

Thursday, November 9th

Made a fine start this morning at 5½ A.M. After about two hours stopped to take in some passengers and 16 bales of

[2]Rev. Anderson is writing about the defeat of Farragut's fleet and General Bank's army in their attempt to push up Red River and take Shreveport. Gould's regiment was recruited in Red River County.

cotton. At 10½ stopped to take in wood. 1 P.M., we are now within 6 miles of Alexandria—no boats passed up to dawn.

Only one chess player on board and I do not like him and will not play. Some card players on board but no gambling. The passengers are not to be compared with those on the *Sciene,* but the boat is far superior.

At 20 minutes to 2 P.M. came to the bar above Alexandria and found a boat on the bar hard and fast. The *Caddo* which passed us was lying there, having arrived about 7 hours before us. There was also a boat ahead of the *Caddo.* All have to wait until the boat gets off the bar. 3 o'clock—the boat on the bar and in the channel has not moved. 11 P.M.—the boat off at 5 and we started down the rapids.[3] The boat grazed on the bottom all the way but it was only a few minutes and we got to Alexandria at sunset. Took in a stock of provisions and at dark started again. Stopped about 8½ and took on a considerable quantity of wood. We will again sail after the moon gets high enough. I think we will get to the Mississippi tomorrow night. All advise one to go to New Orleans as the cheapest and most expeditious route to New York. Started at 1 A.M. and got to Snaggy Point (said to be one of the worst bars on the river).

Friday Morning, November 10th

5 A.M.—We started and are now 15 minutes after starting fast on the bar. After hard pulling we got off this bar at 2 P.M., and we are now on our way for the mouth of the Red River, 110 miles which we will probably reach this night. It is wearisome traveling. No books to read and the company not very select.

---

[3]Rev. Anderson is here describing the Falls of Red River at Alexandria. The falls are described by Olden Lee Barker in his thesis *A Historical Account of Red River* as follows: "There were greater and more permanent obstructions to navigation on the river. Among these was the falls at Alexandria. In 1840 the United States Government undertook the removal of the falls, but work was not completed. The falls were not finally removed until 1880."

Saturday, November 11th

We arrived at the mouth of Red River at 4½ A.M. and now at 7 getting on finely. Arrived at Bayou Sarah at 8 A.M. on the left bank not a house standing near the shore. Walls and chimneys and a few huts mark the place. Waterloo a few miles lower down on the right bank escaped with less damage. Fort Hudson 3 or 4 miles lower presents a miserable appearance. In a beautiful location, only a few of the houses standing. We are 15 miles above Baton Rouge—125 miles from New Orleans.

1 P.M.—We are now opposite Baton Rouge—a rather pretty place but a country generally flat. It does not appear to have suffered a great deal during the War. The State House and Deaf and Dumb Asylum are handsome buildings and would be much improved by a few shade trees. Some few other houses look well from the river, but only a few. Some manufacturing is in progress—I know not of what kind—they are not very extensive. Nearly the whole country in so far as can be seen from the river up to this point from Shreveport seems to be a wilderness grown up with burrs and young cottonwood. Bermuda grass seems to have taken possession of the cultivated farms. A few sugar mills could be seen at work. Until dark little variation in the appearance on the banks of the river, except that we are occasionally passing some fine mansions apparently built in a wilderness.

Sunday Morning, November 12th

Arrived at New Orleans 5 A.M., got off the boat and came to the City Hotel. After breakfast met with Mr. W. H. Gill and W. Bailey. They were in search of L. L. Bailey and Mr. B. H. Epperson. I am going to take a ramble through the city.

Found my overcoat stolen when I went to my room for bed at 8½. Went to the barkeeper. He could do nothing. I had the key in my pocket all day. Went to a Methodist Church and heard a terrible sermon. Went into the Catholic Church— it is a fine building. I rambled about through the city for the afternoon. It is clean and the streets are well kept. The churches and public buildings are of more than ordinary character. Many stores open all day and business in many places little relaxed. Very tired and went to bed at 8½.

Monday, November 13th
   This forenoon went out to purchase cloaks for my children. Can find nothing middling for less than $25 each. Purchased a suit of clothes for myself at $87 in greenback. This embraced overcoat, vest, pantaloons, and a frock coat.
   5 P.M.—Have just got on board the *Olive Branch,* which will take me to Cairo. I paid for a ticket to New York $76.40 greenbacks. Mr. Pearson from Jefferson went off the boat at Convent 60 miles from New Orleans. He came to the city this morning. He told me about a fine young man of the name of Marlie or Marlow (I think from Bonham) when getting off the *Sciene* was drowned by the capsizing of the boat. We are just about to start.

Tuesday, November 14th
   Started yesterday at 5 P.M. Can see little on either bank of the river. Got to Baton Rouge 130 miles at 4½ A.M. Passed Port Hudson 23 miles higher up—Waterloo 6 miles—Bayou Sara 6 miles—Mouth of Red River 40 miles—Fort Adams 17 miles and arrived at Natchez 60 miles higher up—Natchez is 277 miles from New Orleans.We arrived there at 8 P.M. and started for Vicksburg. We passed on the right: Riding, St. Joe, Grand Gulf, Hard Times, New Carthage, and Warrentown. Had to lie up 5 hours in consequence of a very dense fog. We will get to Vicksburg 401 miles above New Orleans this day. We got to Vicksburg at 2 P.M. and, after taking in some freight and passengers, started on our way.

Thursday, November 16th
   Passed the mouth of the Yazoo river at 3 P.M. Yesterday at 5 passed Millikin's Bend.

Vicksburg shows the effects of the war. Not a tree standing near. Nothing attractive in the appearance on the slope of the range of hills along the river. I noticed the spires of 3 of the churches which are uninjured. The courthouse—I suppose—is a beautiful circular building, on the top of a lofty hill. It is surrounded by many lofty white columns which support the roof. The hospital is a long brick building surrounded by the tents of soldiers. There are two or three handsome residences, which seem to have survived the ravages of the war. On the south of the city the slope of the hill is covered with little huts. The whole place is marked with desolation. Indeed, from Baton Rouge up to this point I have seen but 2 or 3 sugar houses left uninjured.

9 A.M.—Passed this evening at 7½ Greenville, 547 miles from New Orleans. At 8½ passed Columbia 10 miles higher up. We are now within a few miles from Gaines Landing which is 575 miles from New Orleans.

Friday, November 17th

9 A.M. Passed Bolivar 30 miles and arrived at Napoleon 15 miles. While landing mail at Napoleon, the boat for Des Arcs was just leaving when a snag ran through her side and came up through the deck. There was a terrible cry as all on board thought the boat was about to sink. The pilot and the engineer left their posts, but it was soon ascertained the snag had entered the boat above the water mark and there was no danger. Passed the mouth of the White River at 9 P.M. Passed Helena this morning before daylight and the mouth of the St. Frances after sunrise. We will get to Memphis 818 miles from New Orleans between 2 and 3 this afternoon. We will then be 259 miles from Cairo.

Arrived at Memphis at 4 P.M.—Put off freight and took on 250 bales of cotton for St. Louis. Did not start till 10 P.M. and Thursday came a few miles through the fog.

Saturday, November 18th
   Passed Randolph and Ashport 40 miles above Memphis.

Sunday, November 19th, 8 A.M.
   We ran till 2 A.M. when the dense fog caused us to stop.
The boat in coming to a landing struck hard against the bank
but no damage was done—took on wood and laid up till 7
o'clock. We are now about 80 miles below Cairo and I fear
we will not arrive in time for the cars[4] to start this day.

*   *   *

   The reverend-professor completed his trip and proved that
a man can go home again under the proper sectarian auspices.
He then returned to his Red River real estate and students and
lived until 1884. He was buried in the old Clarksville Cemetery
near such fellow pioneers as James Clark, Col. Charles De-
Morse, Col. N. C. Gould—the company of whom he approved
more than many he encountered on his river travels. More so
than most, he was prepared to cross the River Styx.

_____

[4]Train.

24.

Reconstruction, Davidson Style

TIME as well as distance separated Washington and Appomattox from the Red River frontier. News and reports came across the land and up and down the rivers slowly, which may have been as well, for without instant communication there were few instant reactions of violence. Men were inclined to say "Well . . .," rather than "Hell . . .!"

Old South romanticism was not characteristic of this frontier. Realism was, so there was less surprise in hearing of Lee's surrender and more practical apprehension of how the transition would affect civil government and protect against interim lawlessness.

In the years 1866 and 1867 a record of sixteen murders went before the grand jury of Red River County, but many more were reported without any indictments.

It became known that a Civil Rights Act had been passed by Congress in April, 1865, and was followed later in 1867 by the Reconstruction Act, which was passed over President Andrew Johnson's veto and implemented by dividing the former Confederacy into five military districts.

It was early in 1868 when people in the Clarksville area heard that a large force of Union soldiers had come from General Phil Sheridan's New Orleans headquarters into Texas under command of Brevet Brigadier General Sheets. A marching force was on its way from Marshall, Texas, to establish garrisons for martial law in the county seat towns.

One afternoon their bugle calls came to the ears of Clarksville citizens. Children ran to their mothers, and the women looked to their men, who looked at each other in grim acceptance of another turn of events.

The detachment camped a half-mile south on what was called the Mt. Pleasant road. Couriers rode into town with orders from Second Lieutenant James Davidson, 11th U.S. Infantry, their commander, that all civil officers of Red River County meet him next morning, 10 A.M., at the district courthouse. It was pointed out that failure to keep this rendezvous would result in immediate removal from office and equally immediate arrest.

And so another pioneer community braced itself, as so many have in the long course of history, to meet a new symbol of authority over it. A descendant of one of those families likened the feeling of his grandparents to that of the Romans in 410 A.D. when Alaric and his Visigoths marched in. The comparison may be on the dramatic side, but it may have had validity for the ex-Confederates who stood on the Clarksville courthouse steps that morning when Lt. Davidson and his two buglers led the soldiers into town and nailed a proclamation of martial law to the courthouse door.

He then had his sergeant take over the Samuel Rhine home on the northeast corner of the square to serve as official headquarters, and the Commercial Hotel was turned into quarters for the soldiers. In both cases the occupants were told to find lodging elsewhere. C'est la guerre.

In the meeting at the courthouse, Lt. Davidson said that he was a soldier with a duty to perform, that he expected cooperation, that the conduct of his command would be correct, fair, and just, but that any misbehavior of the citizens would be severely punished.

At first there were some disorders, but when the ones responsible were arrested and put in the stockade which had been erected on a vacant lot and they were left on a diet of bread and water, the confinement and diet proved thoroughly effective. No serious trouble disturbed the town, the county, or its young Scottish commander who was to have a career as checkered as the plaid of his native clan.

Lt. Davidson was not too happy with his Red River post. In a letter of September 2, 1869, to the Adjutant General of the U.S. Army, Major General E. D. Townsend, the lieutenant asked for transfer to a cavalry regiment in active service against the Indians, stating that he had served in the cavalry in England and preferred that branch of the military.

The request was not granted, for the infantry was not at all inclined to lose a good officer to the cavalry, and the endorsements of his superior officers were all excellent.

This praise, very naturally, was not shared by the civilian population under his command. They did not like him. They would not have liked any Yankee in his position.

In the winter of 1869 the Fifteenth Amendment to the U.S. Constitution was submitted. In the fall term of the District Court of Red River County that year, twenty-two members of the jury included the names of fourteen Negroes. That Lt. Davidson selected those emancipated men with good judgment was proved by the fact that seven of them who were still living as late as 1900 were on record as homeowners and respected citizens. Time was validating law and justice.

As judge in holding court, Davidson's decisions were subject to no appeal. Only one case record in the district court remains to refer to him as "Acting Military Sub-Commissioner for Red River." The records of other cases tried during the years of his judicial authority were not kept.

However, there is other evidence of the impression which he made and left with the people in that Reconstruction

*This picture of Clarksville was taken in 1861
of the southeast corner of the public square.
The fence surrounds the old courthouse where
Lt. Davidson held his public meeting.*

*This Model 38 hand-drawn and hand-operated
piston pumper is similar to the fire engine ordered for Clarksville in 1893, as recounted in
chapter 25. (Picture courtesy of the Howe Fire
Apparatus Company.)*

period. Such examples on the local level as they were lived in towns throughout the Confederate states yield the story of government inability, perhaps of any government anytime anywhere, to cope with the personal relations between those who represent it and those it represents, especially when they are victor and vanquished.

For instance, almost thirty years after the Reconstruction era a Captain J. B. Donoho gave an interview to the *Clarksville News* in June, 1899, and paid his disrespects to the memory of Lt. Davidson in no uncertain terms:

"Davidson, the Federal commander at this place, in whom appeared to center all power, both civil and military, was a despicable character. He had every attribute of the petty tyrant . . . Placed here ostensibly to preserve the peace and protect persons and property, his every aim appeared directed in the way of harassing the ex-Confederates. When an election was held, every man who voted had to first register and pay twenty-five cents and then had to vote at the county seat. There was no other voting place in the county. Davidson's imperial orders directed that voters should come in town and vote; if they had any business to transact to do it and then go straight home and go to work . . . I remember on one occasion Davidson attempted to disarm John Henderson, the quickest and best pistol shot ever seen in this county. Henderson drew his gun and would have killed Davidson had he not fled into the County Clerk's office."

Davidson resigned his commission, and in the spring of 1870 Gov. Davis appointed him Adjutant General and Police Commissioner of Texas. Thus he continued up the ladder of unpopularity. Thirty-five hundred men were recruited for his militia, with most of the arms furnished by the federal government. An Austin newspaper commented, "We predict that General Davidson will make his office anything but a sinecure, and we advise felons, assassins, desperadoes, and their abettors to act, if they are wise, upon the theory that if peace is not kept, somebody will get hurt."

That this prediction was an understatement is borne out by the following excerpts from Norman Kittrell's book. Evidently criminals were not the only objective.

His (Gov. Davis') administration was the most oppressive, tyrannical, and iniquitous ever visited upon a free people. A law was enacted creating a state police force, at the head of which was one James Davidson, a carpetbagger, a pigmy in physical stature, but in moral, or rather immoral depravity, a giant. His police force roamed over Texas, arresting without warrant, robbing, plundering, murdering. They invaded the home of a worthy citizen of Limestone County and robbed him of $3,000. They shot down in cold blood two of the best citizens of Tyler, Smith County.

I saw Adjutant General and Chief of Police Davidson ride into the town of Huntsville about the middle of January, 1871, at the head of a squad of armed state police and post a proclamation declaring martial law and levying a tax of twenty-five cents on the dollar's worth of property to pay the expenses of the unlawful occupation of the town. I know this to be true because I paid part of the tax for my widowed mother . . .[1]

In January 1872, Congress passed the General Amnesty Bill. Obviously the days of the carpetbagger were coming to an end. James Davidson took his cue, nor was that all. In November 1872, he did not appear at his office in Austin. In fact, he could not be located anywhere. Investigation showed that all money belonging to his department was also missing, and it revealed that the sum came to exactly $37,-454.67. A news report at the time contributed the fact that "the labor required to get up the data on his embezzlements so burdened the department that extra clerks had to be added."

Finally it was discovered that Mr. Davidson was treating himself to a very practical vacation. He had skipped the country and gone to Belgium, and since Belgium had no extradition treaty with the United States then, he was safe.

James Davidson, if not the South, was reconstructed and can only be assumed to have lived happily ever after.

---

[1]Norman G. Kittrell, *Governors Who Have Been and other Public Men of Texas* (Houston: Dealy-Elgin Co., 1921)

25.

Fire Engine No. 1

IN every pioneer community the great danger was fire, and the only way it could be fought was with "bucket brigades." These were lines of men who passed buckets of water from one to another from other men drawing water from the nearest wells. The process was slow and so seldom effective that usually all that was left was the lot.

After an 1890 census gave Clarksville a population of 1,588 people, the metropolitan feeling ran high enough to vote to invest in a fire engine which was duly ordered from the Howe Pump and Engine Co. in Indianapolis at an $800 cost.

The firemen were not to be paid, but volunteers were abundant both for the social status involved as well as the fact that there would be exemption from jury duty and the annual "street tax" of $5.00 which was levied on male citizens between 21 and 45 years of age.

Still another attraction was the lure of uniforms, a matter of long slickers and tin hats lettered in flaming red.

On a day in March, 1893, the long and eagerly awaited

engine arrived, and there was no lack of manpower to help unload it at the railway depot. It was indeed the last word in firefighting equipment splendor, though minus any motive power.

Proudly the firemen pulled it to the public square for exhibition, with the fire chief leading the parade with a fireman's axe featuring a blade and big iron spike.

On each side of the engine was a lever to be worked up and down by the firemen to pump the water. This mechanism was exhibited to all who had come to the square, and then the engine was pulled to the new fire station, a shed built next to the jail, more generally referred to as "calaboose." All of this civic complex was in a corner of the Pound Pen, a lot where stray livestock were kept until owners came to claim the animals and pay the proper ransom.

The jailer, one Dan Kirk, was now in charge of the fire station as well as the "pen." He was a man who took all this combined responsibility seriously, and when a citizen once asked him, "If you were to die, what in the world would we do without you?" Mr. Kirk replied that this was his own greatest anxiety.

That evening following the fire engine's arrival, it was decided to have a demonstration of its capabilities on the public square, and this event was announced to take place "at early candle lighting time."

A large goods box was soaked with kerosene, more popularly known as coal oil. This was placed near a well and ignited. Then the firemen in full regalia rushed to the fire station and ran back with the engine. The feed hose was dropped into the well, and the dozen men grabbed the levers and pumped with all their might. The "fire" was extinguished, and everyone applauded the successful operation. Then the men returned the engine to its station and happily went home.

However, a group of pranksters had other plans for later that night. They set fire to some old lumber on a vacant lot on the outskirts of town and then sounded the alarm in the usual way of shooting off pistols and rifles.

At once the firemen jumped out of bed and ran from their homes to get and bring the engine to the false alarm, which nevertheless drained three good wells before it was put out.

Wearily and less happily they went home again. But a few hours later the old Sherry Hotel, a two-story wooden building of pre-Civil War vintage burst into flames, and this time the alarms were shot off with enough ammunition to have supplied the Battle of Shiloh.

In fact, one of the guests in the hotel, a traveling correspondent for the *Louisville Courier Journal,* was so sure that a battle or riot was raging that he hid under his bed and resisted rescue for quite some time.

Later, when he recovered and returned to Kentucky, he wrote a full account of the adventure for his paper there, adding a cartoon of big-hatted men shooting pistols with the caption, "This is the way they give fire alarms in Clarksville, Texas."

But the hotel fire taxed the new engine beyond its strength, as well as the endurance of the firemen. That first night's initiation was too much for man or machine. Seven hundred dollars' worth of fire insurance had to be taken out on the engine itself, and Negro helpers were recruited to give the white brethren a respite.

Other problems followed for the fire alarm system when the state legislature passed a law prohibiting the carrying of concealed weapons and setting a heavy fine. The enforcement officers were on a fee system, and a good part of their earnings came from pistol fines, for most men continued to carry guns.

There was the case of Garrett Igo who was eating supper in a restaurant, heard of a fire, pulled the napkin out of his collar, dashed out, and emptied his Colt .45 into the air. He was promptly arrested by the sheriff and put in jail. The next day he was fined $100 and costs.

Mr. Igo expressed himself in no uncertain terms. "Here I

was trying to do a good turn for this little bobtailed place and this is the gratitude I get. I will never set foot in the corporate limits of Clarksville again. It can all burn down!"

Whereupon he moved across the Red River into Oklahoma and enjoyed fifty years of self-imposed exile with his Colt.

But with or without the pistol alarms, the career of Fire Engine No. 1 went on to put out many a small fire and to fight a losing battle with all the big ones.

EPILOGUE

There is much dust on the old papers in the old boxes which men and women have kept on their land beside the Red River. But when the sunlight is let in, the motes of dust blow away on the river air. And with them is a sound almost as old as the river. It is the sound of ghosts who swagger and sometimes cry and sometimes curse. But most of the time they laugh. And the sound of laughter is man's best accompaniment to history.

CHAPTER SOURCE MATERIAL

1. The Judge's Dilemma
   Newspaper file in E. W. Bowers collection and Minutes of Red River County District Court, Book A, pp. 1-20. 1840
2. Star Navy
   B. C. Jones, W. C. (Tobe) Marchbanks, Albert S. Giddens the Manchester postmaster whose wife was playing the piano at the time of incident. 1902
3. Master and Slave
   Part I
      Cause No. 684 District Court Red River County and "Handbook of Texas"
   Part II
      Ibid., Cause No. 1127
   Part III
      Ibid., Cause No. 899
   1838-45
4. Female Education
   Cause No. 585 District Court Red River County
   1841
5. Confederate Reunions
   Newspaper file in E. W. Bowers collection 1893-1919 and personal interviews of co-author Bowers with Miss Ethel Stanley and Mrs. Vera Smith.
6. Red River Medicine Part I
   Minutes of District Court Red River County, Cause No. 295, 1840.

   Edward Hughart was a member of Wavell's Colony in 1826. The colony was formed by Arthur Goodall Wavell and Benjamin Rush Milam in what was then Red River County but later just over the line in Bowie County. While the colony was under Mexican rule in 1833 Hughart fell in love with a Miss Alderine Berry, but as marriages were not legal unless performed by a Catholic priest, and no priest was available, the couple made a Bond for Marriage which was dated Aug. 18, 1833 and signed by Collin McKinney, George Collom, Collin M. Collom, Wesley Byers (*Handbook of Texas* for sureties on bond). After Texas Independence on March 2, 1836, the marriage was formally and finally recognized. Such procedure happened with many couples in those years.

Part II

Ibid., Cause No. 2708, 1854-56

Part III

Ibid., Cause No. 2039, 1838

Handbook of Texas

7. City With No Mosquitoes

Dr. Nowlin Watson and Byron Black, heads of Mosquito Committee, Clarksville, of which co-author E. W. Bowers was a member, 1920

8. Fairest of the Prairie Flowers

Mrs. F. L. Woodward, great-granddaughter of Caroline Eleanor Collum. Original letters of Caroline Eleanor Sample and Hiram Baker. 1835-45

9. O Tempora, O Mores

Copies of lists of laws owned by Mrs. Jerrold Marx of Clarksville and *The Clarksville Times*. 1840-65

10. Ring Up The Curtain

1874-1908

Diary of William M. Bowers

Letters of Charlie Gaines and Henry Goldberg

City Marshall Brown referred to in the pistol fire alarm incident later became Chief of Police in Dallas. Present Sheriff Bill Decker of Dallas served under him as Deputy Constable.

11. When Carnegie Lost Money

1902-1905

E. W. Bowers, Mrs. Morgan Graves, Mrs. George Whiteman

12. Good For What Ails You

1885-1900

Private letters in E. W. Bowers collection

District Judge N. L. Dalby

Frank X. Tolbert, *Dallas News*

Paris News ad

Co-author Bowers was taken to Dalby Springs as a child for treatment.

13. Christmas 1863
    Private letters E. W. Bowers collection
14. The Mighty Morrill
    1842-58
    District Court Red River County, Cause No. 2121
15. Fun For Free
    1893
    E.W. Bowers, Albert Fowler, Miss Demarious Fowler
    For many years the bridge referred to was called "Sissies Crossing."
    1898 Religious Debate reported by Henry Lennox, Tom Ellis Sr., W. E. Whitener, H. C. (Clay) Bailey
    1884 Swindle Case (never tried) from Minutes of District Court Red River County, also interviews with E. M. Bowers, then District Clerk and father of co-author, H. H. Lennox, C. D. Lennox, Fred Nagle, Will Ligon
16. Politics Texas Style
    Diary of William M. Bowers 1880, 1889, 1892
17. The Sporting Life
    Clarksville Northern Standard, Nov. 6, 1884
    Minutes of District Court Red River County
18. Anchors Aweigh
    1839-1870, Ibid., Cause No. 2711
19. The Iron Horse Comes
    Diary of William M. Bowers 1876
    Texas & Pacific R.R. Co
20. Robert Potter and Lion of the Lakes
    Minutes of District Court Red River County 1842
    American Notes by Charles Dickens
    Diary of Harriet Potter from A. L. Burford, Texarkana, collection
    Newspaper files in E. W. Bowers collection
    Histories included in Bibliography
21. The Hanging Tree
    E. W. Bowers, Capt. J. B. Donoho
22. A Bit of Bigamy 1837-1870
    1837-1870
    Minutes of District Court Red River County
    Mrs. Bonnie Harvey, Houston, descendant of the Bryarly family. The last steamboat to run on Red River was named Bonnie Bell for her.
    Miss Malvina (Bena) Clark, granddaughter of founders of Clarksville

23. River Voyages
        1844 and 1865
        Rev. John Anderson diary from grandson John Anderson
        Handbook of Texas
        Co-author Bowers' father attended Anderson's school
        1849
24. Reconstruction—Davidson Style
        Minutes of District Court Red River County 1870
        Microfilms U.S. War Dept.
        Handbook of Texas
        Newspaper file E. W. Bowers collection
25. Fire Engine No. 1
        1892 Newspaper file E. W. Bowers and interviews
        Howe Pump & Engine Co.

BIBLIOGRAPHY

A. Garland Adair and Ellen Bohlender Coats, *Texas, Its History* (Philadelphia: John C. Winston Co., 1954)

Pat B. Clark, *Clarksville and Old River County* (Dallas: Mathis, Van Nort and Co., 1937)

James M. Day, *The Texas Almanac 1857-1873* (Waco: Texian Press, 1967)

Marion Humphreys Farrow, *Troublesome Times in Texas* (San Antonio: Naylor Company, 1959)

Z. T. Fulmore, *History and Geography of Texas As Told In County Names* (Austin: Steck-Vaughn, 1935)

Herbert and Virginia Gambrell, *A Pictorial History of Texas* (New York; E. P. Dutton and Co., 1960)

William R. Hogan, *The Texas Republic* (Norman, Okla.: University of Oklahoma Press, 1946)

William Moses Jones, *Texas History Carved In Stone* (Houston: Monument Publishing Co., 1958)

L. W. Kemp, *The Signers of the Texas Declaration of Independence* (Houston: Anson Jones Press, 1944)

Norman G. Kittrell, *Governors Who Have Been and Other Public Men of Texas* (Houston: Dealy-Elgin Co., 1921)

Elithe Hamilton Kirkland, *Love Is A Wild Assault* (New York: Doubleday and Company, 1959, 1967)

David Lavender, *The Rockies* (New York: Harper and Row Publishers, 1958)

A. W. Neville, *Red River Valley Then and Now* (Paris, Texas: North Texas Publishing Co., 1948)

Anna J. Hardwicke Pennybacker, *A New History of Texas for Schools* (Tyler, Texas: Privately printed, 1888)

Ernest C. Shearer, *Robert Potter, Remarkable North Carolinian and Texan* (Houston: University of Houston Press, 1951)

Kenneth M. Stampp, *The Pecular Institution, Slavery in the Ante-Bellum South* (New York: Alfred A. Knopf, Inc., 1956)

Diary of William M. Bowers, collection of grandson, Eugene W. Bowers

Handbook of Texas, 2 vols. (Austin: Texas State Historical Association, 1952)

History of Lamar County, (Paris, Texas: North Texas Publishing Co., 1937)

Homer S. Thrall, *Thrall's Texas History.* Bowers collection, date missing, but purchased prior to 1888

Texas Almanac (Dallas: A. H. Bello Corp., 1967)

Northern Standard and *The Standard,* copies of Clarksville newspapers, 1882-1887.

Minutes and Records of County Court of Red River County, 1837-

Southwestern Historical Quarterly (Austin: Texas State Historical Association, 12 years' copies)

Diary of Harriet Potter, from A. L. Burford collection.

Diary of Rev. John Anderson, from grandson, John Anderson.

U.S. War Department microfilm.